IMMERSED IN HIM

L. Emerson Ferrell

Voice Of The Light Ministries

Voice Of The Light Ministries

Published by   Voice of The Light Ministries
              P.O. Box 3418, Ponte Vedra, Florida 32004, USA
              www.voiceofthelight.com

ISBN   978-1-9331-6323-9

TABLE OF CONTENTS

INTRODUCTION

Immersed In Him describes the journey by which man becomes one with The Living Christ. This book will reconnect you with your intended purpose and power of Christianity. The excitement you felt after first meeting Christ will penetrate your soul again with waves of enthusiasm, which may have been buried in form and tradition.

This book describes in very simple but profound ways His principals for change. It is my desire for a transformation to begin in your life. You will be armed with the most fundamental revelations to become the new creature in Christ. I believe the words *born again* have been wrongly taught and consequently negate the transcending dominance of Christ and His Kingdom.

Those who are "born into Christ" must be baptized into the Godhead to complete the transition designed and modeled by Jesus Christ. The transformation is real and your life will change if you allow the Spirit to speak to you as you read.
Those who need help and have tried religion without success, will be renewed by the revelations in this book. The passions of Christ will energize those who are desperately looking for answers to live in these troubling times.

Each chapter will transport your spirits to a new level of understanding and wisdom designed to expose you to light not seen before. God's word was written to train you to rule and reign over all of your circumstances. The difficulties most people are facing is because of wrong thinking.

Jesus only taught one message. Repent, for The Kingdom of God is NOW. "Change the way you think" is one of the definitions of repent. No one, and I mean no one can enter The Kingdom of God without the mind's radical restructure.

Those of you who are not content with yesterday's revelation of Christ will receive new tools to find fresh manna each day. In addition, it will provide each of you who are courageous enough to study it, the power to kick the devil out of your lives once and for all and live victoriously.

The power Christ left His Church has not passed away nor has it been depleted over time. His power, designated for you, is far above the circumstances causing you pain. Now you can destroy the works of the enemy and take back everything you have lost. The revelations in this book are designed to restore shattered destinies and will empower you with that knowledge.

Read this book as often as necessary to see the mysteries you have been given IN Christ. This is not a cliché or another philosophy book. This is the revolutionary tool your spirit has been groaning to receive. Paul says in Romans:

> *We know that all creation has been groaning with the pains of childbirth up to the present time.*
>
> *However, not only creation groans. We, who have the Spirit as the first of God's gifts, also groan inwardly. We groan as we eagerly wait for our adoption, the freeing of our bodies ‹from sin›.*

We were saved with this hope in mind. If we hope for something we already see, it's not really hope. Who hopes for what can be seen?

But if we hope for what we don't see, we eagerly wait for it with perseverance.

Romans 8:22-25 GW

The birth Paul is speaking about is the true *Born Again* experience, which has become more of a religious saying than a transformation. This is your time for a true experience with the lover of your soul and the One who purchased you before the foundation of the world. You were created to walk in the righteousness, peace and joy of the Holy Ghost. Do not miss this day of visitation.

Everything is yours to receive because it is the pleasure of your heavenly Father to GIVE you His Kingdom. Receive it now.

CHAPTER 1

REVELATION
OF GENESIS

The Lord has given me grace to fast solid foods extended periods of time over the past several years. During those times I experienced, for lack of a better word, "trances." Peter is said to have had this type of experience in Acts 11:5, *"I was in the city of Joppa praying; and in a trance I saw a vision..."*

This particular vision began with my standing inside a large bubble constructed from a material that resembled liquid light. In other words, it was as bright as the noonday sun but transparent and flexible without being wet. I remember feeling joyfully overwhelmed by the presence of the Holy Spirit. My mind was peaceful but actively alert with a sense of "knowing" without having to be taught.

Instantly, my spirit was flooded with images and sounds unfamiliar to anything I had ever encountered. The Holy Spirit spoke and my whole being felt as though it was electrically charged. His voice flooded over me like Niagara Falls in surround sound. *"Creation is the heavenly model for all transformations"*, He said.

Immediately, my mind was submerged in total darkness that moved like a wave in every direction at the same time. The absence of light made it impossible to see, but the presence of vast emptiness was scary. Nevertheless, I remained peaceful but aware of my frightening surroundings.

Suddenly, I felt helpless and hopeless as though empty space was swallowing me. I felt a sensation of chaos and confusion consuming me like a "black hole" beyond the reach of God. My mind was gripped with terror and fear. I cried out from within the depths of my spirit for Jesus to help me. Instantly I was transported out of darkness and standing beside God the Father, Son and Holy Spirit. I understood at that moment the Fear of God and what eternity without Him would be like. The images were so vivid and remarkable that to this day it makes me tremble.

The next thing I witnessed was Jesus singing over the same dark empty space from which I was just rescued. Almost instantaneously I knew I was reliving the creation from inside the mind of God. The empty void began to fill with His amazing voice as the substance of love and beauty, which I sensed to be living water.

The next image I saw was the outline of the Holy Spirit in the shape of a dove resting over the entire body of water. Suddenly, an explosion erupted from The Father, which lit up the entire universe with a blinding light greater than millions of nuclear detonations. The power from His utterance sent atomic vibrations over the Spirit and into the water, which formed the galaxies, stars and planets, including earth.

The Holy Spirit spoke and said, *"Creation is the method, which God uses to transform death and darkness into life and light.*

It is the design for transforming man as well as universes. Time is only relevant in the physical world, therefore, during creation God completed all things in Christ who was and is and is to come. The love of God finishes everything before He begins as nothing is left to chance.

The scriptures from Genesis to Revelation is the manifold wisdom of God hidden in Christ outside of time and space revealed to those whose temporal natures have abandoned their desires. "

He went on to say, *"Creation is ever expanding in Christ."* In other words, I thought, we have the opportunity each day to recreate heaven on earth using the model of Genesis in conjunction with the manifestations of the Godhead.

The Spirit continued, *"The Water, Spirit and Blood are the spiritual mixture of heaven and earth, which establishes Gods Kingdom with power on earth, as it is in heaven."*

The Holy Spirit finished by saying, *"The Water and The Spirit are the spiritual forces over sin, sickness and death and they reside IN HIM. All power has been given and those with eyes to see and ears to hear will do the greater works."*

This book is the result of many such visitations and visions from the Spirit. Jesus says in the book of Revelation, *I am the First and the Last, says the Lord God who is and was and is to come, the Ruler of all.* Therefore, in Bible chronology, He would be the Genesis and Revelation and everything in between.

The words Jesus spoke are the principles I live and use to understand the scriptures. Scripture primarily describes Christ from two perspectives. The first is the physical model of the Son of Man and the last is the spiritual authority over all things on earth and in heaven. Both descriptions are relevant if our desire is to be like Him.

Genesis describes heavenly elements that were used to create the visible world and are still connected with the invisible realm. These elements were designed to support both physical and spiritual life and are light, water and blood.

> *For there are three that bear record in heaven, the Father, the Word, and the Holy Ghost: and these three are one.*
> *And there are three that bear witness in earth, the Spirit, and the water, and the blood: and these three agree in one.*
>
> *1 John 5:7-8 KJV*

John understood The Christ better than anyone including Paul. His account of the heavenly dimension could not be described with the languages of man, as you may understand after reading Revelation. Nevertheless, he was able to connect heaven and earth together very well in these verses. The elements, as we will learn, are a picture of Christ, both physical and spiritual.

> *This is he who came by water and by blood, Jesus Christ; not by water only but by water and by blood.*
>
> *1 John 5:6 BBE*

Jesus was the Son of Man because of water but He was the Son of God because of His blood. Jesus was, is and will be for all eternity because He is the physical body, which contains the living water and His Fathers blood. The Holy Spirit was the witness to this everlasting truth before the foundation of the world.

And the Spirit is the witness, because the Spirit is true.

1 John 5:7 BBE

The elements of creation are keys to the mind of God. The Holy Spirit will illuminate all those who are willing to submit to His "ways."

In the beginning God created the heavens and the earth.

The earth was formless and void, and darkness was over the surface of the deep, and the Spirit of God was moving over the surface of the waters.

Then God said, Let there be light; and there was light.

Genesis 1:1-3 NASB

God created the Earth from a formless, empty, dark abyss. The description is very powerful when you consider God used His imagination as the blueprint for the origin of all things. But the reason He created it and man's role has been discussed for centuries. I believe love to be the answer, but the world's concept of love has been the stumbling block.

God is Love and the Father of "The Truth." The combination of love and truth empowers creativity and multiplication. Truth and love are the substances, which form the creative mind of God and it is the reason the devil is unable to create.

Love is the greatest authority and power in the universe, which God demonstrated by sacrificing His only Son. We were created to emulate our Father and surrender to Him because of His great love. If we don't, our life will have been for naught.

> *The first commandment is you shall love the Lord your God with all your heart, and with all your soul, and with all your mind, and with all your strength.*

> *The second is this, you shall love your neighbor as yourself. There is no other commandment greater than these.*

> *Mark 12:30-31 NASB*

Religion demands its followers to submit to commandments and regulations in order to be accepted by "God." Jesus reduced all of man's religious obligations into one, love. But man's rebellious nature refuses to love anyone but himself and it is this nature, which is the source of all man's fear.

satan is the enemy of love and the source of fear. The Spirit of Love destroys fear because it is wrapped in faith and unleashed by our submission.

A. THE FREQUENCY OF LOVE IS FAITH

Frequency is most often used when describing the number of times certain events happen, such as someone buying coffee or grocery shopping. It is also used when measuring light, sound and electromagnetic waves. I believe in order to understand the authority we have as spiritual beings, we must become more acquainted with terminology most often used in scientific discussions. For our purposes, frequencies of electromagnetic waves and vibrations as they pertain to light and sound will be our focus.

Love is the frequency of His Glory, which sustains all life and removes darkness. God speaks and from His innermost being resounds the Word of His love, Jesus. **Jesus is the song of love The Father sings over all creation. Love is the nature and vibration that holds all things together.**

All of creation groans to hear the sound of His love sung over them. **Jesus is God's frequency of love vibrating at the speed of light changing everything that hears His voice. The sound of His voice is the life and light of all energy.**

The sound of love is the vibration of creation. The Father's song is love and it is the harmony that holds all things in place.

Love provoked God to create life from the shapeless, empty, void of the universe. It is His longing for all things to experience His love in righteousness and peace. Love is the substance of His consciousness and what produces His thoughts.

For I am conscious of my thoughts about you, says the Lord, thoughts of peace and not of evil, to give you hope at the end.

Jeremiah 29:11 BBE

Love is one of the most commonly used words around the world. Indeed, it is spoken in every language and culture especially with couples that marry.

The United States reports one in two marriages end in divorce demonstrating love does not necessarily mean commitment. The sad fact is, love is most often used to express an emotion or feeling.

The well-known cliché, God is Love, describes the character of our heavenly Father. But it is much deeper than that. God is Spirit and during my visitations in His presence, the garments that clothed Him would best be described as light knitted together with threads of love. It was these threads of love, which prevented the light of His holy Glory from burning me up.

The Love of God is not an emotion or a feeling but the Spirit of all life. Love is the energy that sustains life. We are created to love, thereby procreating life because we are from God. Life is the byproduct of God's Love and it originated from the invisible world or spiritual realm.

God is Spirit, making it difficult to locate Him with our senses. The five senses commonly used to determine reality are inadequate. The following verse is one reason I focus primarily on the words of Christ.

Life is spiritual. Your physical existence doesn't contribute to that life. The words that I have spoken to you are spiritual. They are life.

John 6:63 GW

16

God's desire is for Sons who will love and serve Him because they have experienced the reality of the spiritual realm. Those who have learned the language of love must be skilled in waiting on His presence without preconceived ideas or desires. Faith is the gift of God to those who love Him.

And without faith it is not possible to be well-pleasing to Him, for it is necessary for anyone who comes to God to have the belief that God is, and that he is a rewarder of all those who make a serious search for Him.

Hebrews 11:6 BBE

Now faith is the substance of things hoped for, and the sign that the things not seen are true.

Hebrews 11:1 BBE

Faith may be defined as the substance of things unseen but with the conviction and assurance of its reality. Love is the power source of faith. If your faith is not working, it may be because the love you confess is more emotional and centered primarily around your needs. Love and faith originate within God and are the substance of His mercy and grace located in Jesus. In order to manifest faith we must be rooted and grounded "in" love.

and that Christ may dwell in your hearts through faith, as you are being rooted and grounded in love.

Ephesians 3:17 NRSV

But now abide faith, hope, love, these three; but the greatest of these is love.

1 Corinthians 13:13

The connection between love and faith are undeniable. God's words are spiritual by nature and unless used in that context the results will be ordinary. I am defining ordinary as a life, which is unable to demonstrate the supernatural power of God, which means living unaffected by fear and disease.

I believe most people acknowledge the existence of something beyond the visible realm. The physical world was designed to reflect the spiritual not vice versa. The invisible world is genuine but faith is the language we must use.

Reality is faith, but the only way to demonstrate it is love.

God deposited a part of His Spirit in all men, in order for us to experience His love. He is the Father of all spirits.

Then they threw themselves down with their faces to the ground and said, O God, the God of the spirits of all people, will you be angry with the whole community when only one man sins?

Numbers 16:22 NET

Let the LORD, the God of the spirits of all humankind, appoint a man over the community,

Numbers 27:16 NET

The reason so many question God's existence is because they refuse to love others more than themselves. As a result they are unaware of God's Spirit knocking at their hearts door.

He has deposited in our spirits a measure of faith clothed in love. Once we give our love away without expecting something in return, the faith in that love engages heaven on our behalf. This is not a physical recipe for touching God but a heavenly key to unlock its treasures.

> *And if I have the gift of prophesy, and know all mysteries and all knowledge; and if I have all faith, so as to remove mountains, but do not have love I am nothing.*
>
> *1 Corinthians 13:2*

The spiritual nature of God is undeniable and His words, thoughts and actions must be understood from that perspective if we are to experience the full impact of His love.

If we cry out for His Spirit to touch our spirits we will have an experience beyond our senses, which will release an indescribable love. His love will create a desire to know Him, which is accessed by faith. The more we love, the more faith we release and the more He releases for us to give back to Him. Do you see how they are connected?

God created the universe and man because of His unsearchable love towards us. He deposited His faith in us to reproduce the same model on earth, as in His Kingdom. The following prayer demonstrates the power of heaven over earth's circumstances.

*Let your kingdom come. Let your pleasure be done,
as in heaven, so on earth.*

*Give us this day bread for our needs.
And make us free of our debts, as we have made
those free who are in debt to us.*

*And let us not be put to the test, but keep us safe
from the Evil One.*

Matthew 6:9-13 BBE

The early Church understood the spiritual realm and His Kingdom to a much greater degree than most do today. Today, "kingdom" is the latest "buzzword" in many churches, but the doctrines of men are promoted, instead of the spiritual principles of Christ. *i agree*

Man generally makes the assumption he and God think alike. Isaiah knew differently and said, *"For My thoughts are not your thoughts, nor are your ways My ways, says the LORD. For as the heavens are higher than the earth, so are my ways higher than your ways, and my thoughts than your thoughts.* (Isaiah 55:8-9).

God forms His decisions from love and manifests them into our world by faith. Man's current mental condition is incapable of understanding God's Kingdom principles and as a result, interprets them religiously. The power of love has been reduced to laws and doctrines negating the supernatural power in Christ and His Kingdom.

Love is the frequency of God, which separates darkness from light. It will produce wholeness or sound doctrine. Paul used

20

the word sound many times to illustrate the mental condition necessary to attract heaven.

Hold to the standard of sound teaching that you have heard from me, in the faith and love that are in Christ Jesus.

2 Timothy 1:13 NRSV

For the time will come when they will not endure sound doctrine; but wanting to have their ears tickled, they will accumulate for themselves teachers in accordance to their own desires,

2 Timothy 4:3 NASB

The frequency of the spiritual realm is different from the sound of the visible realm. The heavenly vibration is a melody of love because the faith of our Lord has overcome.

B. VISIBLE AND INVISIBLE REALMS

We believe the visible world is real because we can access it with our senses. In other words, if we can touch, taste, smell, see or hear it we assume it is "real."

However, science reports the average person is aware or conscious of their environment only six to ten seconds every minute. Think of the implications of that statement, at least for the next ten seconds.

Furthermore, although our brain processes up to 400 billion bits of information a second we are only aware of 2000. That means we are neither conscious of nor do we perceive most of the environment in the visible world.

21

So even if we could judge reality with our senses huge gaps of information would still be missing.

Picture a lion walking around in his cage at the zoo. The animal is oblivious to anything outside the range of his senses. That analogy might give us some insight into the limited amount of information we use to determine our world. That may partially explain the insatiable appetite human beings have for entertainment.

We are spirit beings first and foremost and even though we temporarily have physical bodies, we must understand some basic principles.

The physical world was created for us to demonstrate our ability to master both realms by relying on our spiritual natures. We lost our way through Adam's disobedience but with the help of the Holy Spirit, we will rediscover together the way to reconnect to our heritage.

God has established laws and principles to sustain the visible and invisible realms, not to restrict His authority or movements. He made a covenant with Abraham to prove His commitment to the visible realm. He knew man was incapable of keeping his promise so God made covenant with Himself. God was not dependent on man because He finished all things inside Christ before the foundation of the world and revealed it to Abraham in the spiritual realm.

Your forefather Abraham was extremely happy at the hope and prospect of seeing My day (My incarnation); and he did see it and was delighted.

John 8:56 AMP

God showed Abraham the completion of all things inside Christ. God united the eternal with the temporal IN CHRIST when He formed the end from the beginning. Let that sink into your spirit.

Everything, which is and was and is to come, happened before time. He uses times and seasons in order to train us for spiritual dimensions. *ci believe this*

I am the Alpha and the Omega, the Beginning and the End, says the Lord God, He Who is and Who was and Who is to come, the Almighty.

> *Revelation 1:8 AMP*

*In other words, **in Christ** God was reconciling the world to Himself, not counting people's trespasses against them, and he has given us the message of reconciliation.*

> *2 Corinthians 5:19 NET, Author's Emphasis*

Eternity lives in God not the other way around. Eternity itself was created by God and its laws were established to sustain the work of the ages completed before the foundation of this earth. The laws He created were to preserve man and demonstrate His love.

C. GODHEAD AND CREATION

In the beginning of the Bible we find the world before the Godhead intervened. The condition of the earth described in Genesis, is the picture of man's spiritual condition before being truly *born again*.

The earth was formless and void, and darkness was over the surface of the deep, and the Spirit of God was moving over the surface of the waters.

Genesis 1:2 NKJV

Jesus answered and said to him, Verily, verily, I say to thee, Except a man be born again, he cannot see the kingdom of God.

John 3:3 KJV

The Spirit of God in verse two of Genesis is described in various ways "moving" over the water. One translation portrays Him as a "wind from God," while others describes Him as fluttering or brooding. It would appear from the descriptions He is imparting or releasing something into the surface of the waters.

For instance, some people describe an invisible sensation "like electricity" moving over their bodies after prayer. Many of these are healed and delivered from sickness or emotional illness after those experiences.

Why would the Holy Spirit be involved in creating the earth and what is He releasing? The importance of those questions is best understood after examining the characteristics of the Godhead.

God the Father, Son and Holy Spirit are three separate Persons with individual characteristics or personalities described as the Godhead. There is no jealousy or competition among the three because they are all one.

Let this mind be in you, which was also in Christ Jesus: Who, being in the form of God, thought it not robbery to be equal with God:

Philippians 2:5-6

We said earlier, God the Father, Son and Holy Spirit created eternal laws and principles to govern the visible and invisible realms. Each One of the Godhead is wholly God and specifically empowered to manifest the Kingdom of God.

The characteristics of each personality in the Godhead are more spectacular than words can describe. I have personally encountered the majestic splendor of God while being paralyzed in the waves of love from the Holy Spirit. Just the recollection of that experience brings tears to my eyes.

It is difficult to explain the amazing sensitivity of the Holy Spirit to anyone who has not encountered His tenderness. A childhood memory may help to illustrate His amazing love.

I recall as a child watching my mother spend hours repairing a hole in my favorite shirt. The shirt was so old and faded that even finding the right color thread took hours. But she would labor over that shirt because she knew how much it meant to me. That is a small picture of the attention and tenderness the Holy Spirit showers on those the Father loves.

He sustains us regardless of our character and disposition towards Him or God. He is the breath we breathe and the life we so often take for granted. In fact, He was the breath God blew into the nostrils of Adam to make his soul alive.

As a side note, my spiritual mind was renewed after I learned to inhale His breath. He only exhales and He has taught me the secrets of the breath of God.

His qualities, although much more gentle, remind us of our earthly mothers. The account in Genesis of "brooding" over the waters depicts a mother hen about to give birth to her chicks.

A mother is one who rarely gives up on those she bares and defends them at all costs. She is the one who will give her life to sustain the lives of her children and those she loves. These marvelous characteristics are some of the ways of the precious Holy Spirit.

The Godhead is the majestic plan of God designed to change the triune nature of man into a living tabernacle. Man has three parts and the purpose of the Godhead is to minister and immerse each part of man into each of His characters.

The buildings of religion were not designed to be God's residence. We are the living, breathing expression of His infinite love and power housed in clay.

For the invisible things of him from the creation of the world are clearly seen, being understood by the things that are made, even his eternal power and Godhead; so that they are without excuse.

Romans 1:20

From the creation of the world, God's invisible qualities, his eternal power and divine nature, have been clearly observed in what he made. As a result, people have no excuse.

Romans 1:20 NASB

And do not grieve the Holy Spirit of God [do not offend or vex or sadden Him], by Whom you were sealed (marked, branded as God's own, secured) for the day of redemption (of final deliverance through Christ from evil and the consequences of sin).

Ephesians 4:30 AMP

God's Spirit is assigned to impregnate our spirits with the incorruptible seed to be born into God's Kingdom. The birth process takes nine months in the natural; it can take years in the spirit. The Holy Spirit sends angels to watch over those who have been marked to ensure their birth into The Kingdom.

D. THE WORD AND THE LIGHT

If love is the motivation for God to create, and faith is the power to transform, what is the image He uses to change empty darkness into reality? What likeness best displays heaven?

The Word and Light are heavens image and likeness to bridge heaven and earth. Light is seen and the Word is heard because it produces waves of energy, which vibrate at frequencies receptive to our eyes and ears.

Likewise, there are frequencies and vibrations beyond our ability to perceive in the natural, but are the foundation and structures for the invisible realm.

The spiritual world moves at speeds faster than light and sound. In fact, I believe the spiritual dimension moves at the speed of thought.

That is why for me the prophetic is so important. God spoke at those frequencies when He created the world, but He knew the results before speaking.

Before returning to Genesis we will examine the Gospel of John, in order to understand the origin of The Word.

> *IN THE beginning [before all time] was the Word (Christ), and the Word was with God, and the Word was God Himself.*

> *He was present originally with God.*

> *All things were made and came into existence through Him; and without Him was not even one thing made that has come into being.*

> *In Him was Life, and the Life was the Light of men.*

> *And the Light shines on in the darkness, for the darkness has never overpowered it.*

> *John 1:1-5 AMP*

The Bible tells us specifically who and where Jesus was before the earth was created. Jesus is not only the Word, but He is the Light of life. Man's physical life originates at birth but men must choose the light, which is Jesus, to live everlastingly with the Godhead.

The truth of the verses in John is made abundantly clear in the following scriptures:

The lamp of the body is the eye; if therefore your eye is clear, your whole body will be full of light.

But if your eye is bad, your whole body will be full of darkness. If therefore the light that is in you is darkness, how great is the darkness.

Matthew 6:22-23 NASB

Your eye is the lamp of your body; when your eye (your conscience) is sound and fulfilling its office, your whole body is full of light; but when it is not sound and is not fulfilling its office, your body is full of darkness.

Be careful, therefore, that the light that is in you is not darkness.

Luke 11:34-35 AMP

There have been many philosophers whose search for God and "truth" was genuine, such as Confucius, Buddha and Gandhi, to name a few. Their works and philosophies brought light to many but it was unable to defeat death.

Jesus is the only life with "The" light, which overcomes death. All philosophies end at the grave, but those who are *born again* will overcome the grave, death and hell. Jesus will forever be the only one capable of offering anyone the light of life for eternity.

John continues by saying, everything created was because of Jesus and nothing has "being" without His consent. Adam became a "living being" because of God's breath of life, which contains the life and light of Christ.

29

All things were made and came into existence through Him; and without Him was not even one thing made that has come into being.

John 1:3 AMP

Then the Lord God formed man from the dust of the ground and breathed into his nostrils the breath or spirit of life, and man became a living being.

Genesis 2:7 AMP

God ensured His legal authority over eternity with the innocent blood of Jesus, which carries the light and life of God. Thereby, satisfying His conditions for righteousness and holiness. His eternal love would sustain all life now and forevermore without any reprisal. His Kingdom is from everlasting to everlasting because of His righteousness.

God sent his Son into the world, not to condemn the world, but to save the world.

Those who believe in him won't be condemned. But those who don't believe are already condemned because they don't believe in God's only Son.

This is why people are condemned: **The light came into the world.** *Yet, people loved the dark rather than the light because their actions were evil.*

People who do what is wrong hate the light and don't come to the light. They don't want their actions to be exposed.

But people who do what is true come to the light so that the things they do for God may be clearly seen.

John 3:17-21 GWORD, Author's Emphasis

The world is condemned because people refuse to accept the perfect Son of God and receive His Light. The world loves darkness and hates light. That rejection produces a mentality whose thoughts are constructed from darkness and illusion.

The master of illusion is the devil. He corrupts light through the use of shadows. Remember, lucifer was "the light bearer" before he was thrown out of heaven. That means he knows how to "twist" and pervert light, creating the illusions so many believe. Those who believe his lies and illusions manifest sin, sickness and death. God does not curse those people; they destroy themselves with greed, selfishness and hate because they love darkness.

Those whose deeds are good and performed in the light open their hearts and understanding to God's goodness. The world does not need religion and more churches it needs to be exposed to the true light of Christ. i agree

In every nation he that fears Him, and works righteousness, is acceptable to Him.

Acts 10:35 ASV

In Genesis, we identified the Holy Spirit "brooding" over the waters and in the following verse God says, "Let there be light and there was light or paraphrasing; Jesus (The Word) The Light be and He Is.

The earth was formless and void, and darkness was over the surface of the deep, and the Spirit of God was moving over the surface of the waters.

Then God said, Let there be light; and there was light.

Genesis 1:2-3 NASB

God speaks The Word, which is The Light or Jesus, into the Holy Spirit, who then impregnates the earth with the incorruptible seed of Christ.

Notice God speaks the words "light be" in the present tense or the proper grammar would be "light is." God does not say light will be or has been: He speaks in the present tense. Remember when He told Moses to tell Pharaoh to say, "I Am" sent me?

Creation is "the" key to understanding the spiritual realm and the true spiritual conversion called *born again.* After God spoke, "Light is," the entire world was impregnated with His Glory. **The earth became the womb, pregnant with God's image and likeness.**

Today, the earth is once again travailing as a woman in childbirth for spiritual sons to be manifested so she can be filled with Christ's Sons forever.

For all creation, gazing eagerly as if with outstretched neck, is waiting and longing to see the manifestation of the sons of God.

*For we know that the whole of Creation is groaning
together in the pains of childbirth until this hour.*

Romans 8:19-22 WEY

Science uses a word called bandwidth to describe
electromagnetic radiation waves. The waves are frequencies of
light vibrating at different speeds producing a spectrum of light
from infrared to ultraviolet. The bandwidth is best illustrated
by looking at a rainbow.

I believe when God said "Light Be," He released His full
bandwidth of glory into the universe through the Holy Spirit
and Jesus.

*And one cried to another and said, Holy, holy, holy
is the Lord of hosts; the whole earth is full of His glory!*

Isaiah 6:3 AMP

In other words, the Godhead released thanksgiving, power,
might, riches, wisdom, strength, honor, glory and blessing into
all creation. Each word describes the likeness and image of
God. This is the glory of God beginning at Genesis spoken of
in Isaiah and culminating at the throne in Revelation.

*And in loud voices they were singing, "It is fitting
that the Lamb which has been offered in sacrifice
should receive all power and riches and wisdom and
might and honor and glory and blessing.*

Revelation 5:12 WEY

33

Amen! (So be it!) they cried. Blessing and glory and majesty and splendor and wisdom and thanks and honor and power and might [be ascribed] to our God to the ages and ages (forever and ever, throughout the eternities of the eternities)! Amen! (So be it!)

Revelation 7:12 AMP

When God said, "light be," He was not creating the sun, moon or stars that happened on the fourth day. He was illuminating the universe with the glory of Christ. God was imparting form and substance into the once dark formless empty mass. He fertilized the visible world with the power to transform mortality to immortality. **He released that power through the Holy Spirit into the water.**

The Bible says all things were created by, for and through Jesus. In other words, without Christ nothing visible or invisible would exist. The completion of all that was, is and is to come began and finished with "light be."

For in him all things in heaven and on earth were created, things visible and invisible, whether thrones or dominions or rulers or powers—all things have been created through him and for him. He himself is before all things, and in him all things hold together.

Colossians 1:16-17 KJV

If we were to imagine the inside of God's mind, I believe it would resemble the awesome beauty and vastness of space. Man outside of Christ will never understand the wonders of the universe. The mysteries of the cosmos are available to those who **enter Christ and His Kingdom.**

Jesus answered him, (Nicodemus) I assure you, most solemnly I tell you, that unless a person is born again (anew, from above), he cannot ever see (know, be acquainted with, and experience) the kingdom of God.

John 3:3 AMP

Those who have eyes to see and spiritual ears to hear what the Spirit is saying will rejoice in the revelation God is releasing in this season. God said, "light be" and released the end and the beginning simultaneously.

Everything was completed at that instant outside of time and space. In Gods mind, the next image is around the throne in heaven with His entire heavenly host worshipping Christ Jesus.

The spiritual world is real and eternal. The spirit of man understands eternity and has the ability to access that dimension now.

Of course, you are alive today in a physical body with "perceived" needs. The word perceived is very important to understand because as we have discovered, **reality is faith**, not feelings. Perceptions are the result of our senses and we will learn they are not an accurate indicator of reality.

The circumstances you may be overwhelmed with today, as realistic as they may seem, have been defeated. The conditions you may be experiencing today are the result of choices made from a lack of understanding.

Does that mean your condition is hopeless and unless Jesus returns from heaven your life will be spent in misery? Absolutely not!

During a 40 day fast, the Holy Spirit showed me a vision that changed my life. He drew back a curtain and allowed me to see the exact moment in time Jesus released His Spirit and descended into hell. I simultaneously saw the physical and spiritual dimensions.

I remember seeing the underworld nervous, confused, and extremely agitated. Jerusalem reflected the same hysteria I was watching in hell. Suddenly, a huge angel appeared between heaven and earth with a key in one hand and a chain in the other.

The heavens were filled with white horses and angels carrying trumpets and spears. They threw the spears into the earth and blew their trumpets. The sound created an earthquake and the spears opened the heavens above the earth to receive revelation and power like lightening.

Suddenly, I heard the large angel scream, "Babylon has fallen," as he chained the devil and unlocked prison cells of those Jesus commanded him to free. The next picture I saw was that of a city resembling Jerusalem crumbling down along with a huge temple.

Instantly, I heard a voice that reminded me of lightening and thunder say, *"It is finished, the One Who is and Was and Is to come has completed all things in time, outside of time and before time. The plans are finished before they began in time and the power over all things resides "in Christ" and is given to those with understanding."*

I saw a lion and a lamb standing above time and space holding a golden book, brighter than one million suns. The lion spoke like a lamb and the lamb walked like a lion. Each page was empty until I saw and heard them speak. As they spoke the pages displayed their words.

I asked the Holy Spirit to explain the vision. He said, *"Those in Christ are His books of life and the pages are empty because His Sons have not written their revelation of Him."* I asked why? He replied, *"They have been preoccupied with other men's ideas and interpretations instead of searching for themselves."* He told me, *"The world is hungry for fresh manna and those willing to pay the price to "Know" Me will fill my books on earth and in heaven."*

Furthermore, He said, *"Live on earth clothed in the blood of His cross and crowned with the knowledge of God's champion."* He said, *"Those who have been reunited with Him by the Spirit and Water had already died the first death and must live unafraid, unattached and outside time.*

He said, *"Religious people are frightened, making their interpretation of the scriptures, particularly "the end times," hopeless and void of the truth.*

Anyone, who is in Christ, has authority over the devil and influence in heaven. Those the devil destroys are ignorant because they feed on the fruit from the tree of the knowledge of good and evil. Stop eating the fruit and listen to my Spirit. My desire is that none should perish."

He revealed Christ to me as the waters of creation and much, much more, some of which I will write in this book.

In Genesis, the Holy Spirit was "brooding" over the waters before God spoke. Water is a heavenly element and is very important to earth, man and God. In the following section we will discover the physical importance, as well as the spiritual.

E. WATER, A HEAVENLY ELEMENT

Day two through six of creation is the meticulous design of God to sow the DNA of Christ into every part of the universe. God separated the water from the water and doing so guaranteed the water and Spirit would operate at every level in the visible world.

> *And God said, Let there be a firmament [the expanse of the sky] in the midst of the waters, and let it separate the waters [below] from the waters [above].*

> *And God made the firmament [the expanse] and separated the waters which were under the expanse from the waters which were above the expanse. And it was so.*
>
> *Genesis 1:6-7 AMP*

Jesus told Nicodemus the water and Spirit were required to be *born again* and thus, see His Kingdom.

Perhaps, one of the most important parts of our discussion will be about water. Man cannot live without it, nor is he able to recreate it cost effectively. Science is able to join hydrogen and oxygen together to form water, but the chemical compound H_2 is not available in earth's atmosphere because of gravity.

The process to extract hydrogen from methane would require extraordinary amounts of natural gas and energy. So theoretically, man can produce water but because of the expense prefers to use other methods.

I believe for obvious reasons, waters origin and source is heaven. Furthermore, I believe the scriptures will demonstrate an amazing comparison between water and Jesus.

And the earth was without form, and void; and darkness was upon the face of the deep: and the Spirit of God moved upon the face of the waters.

Genesis 1:2 WEB

The first thing to notice in this verse is there are two faces, which I believe to be a description of God and Jesus. The first is the nature "darkness" and the second is water.

I know God is light and there is no darkness in Him, but this type of darkness does not represent absence of light. It is the way He masks Himself in order to protect man from His Glory. God is a consuming fire and conceals Himself in the thick smoke of darkness because of His great love.

*The people stayed at a distance, and Moses drew near to the thick **darkness** where God was.*

Exodus 20:21 WEB, Author's Emphasis

*These words **the LORD spoke** to all your assembly on the mount **from the midst** of the fire, of the cloud, and **of the thick darkness**, with a great voice: and he added no more. And he wrote them in two tables of stone, and delivered them to me.*
*And it came to pass, when ye heard the voice from the midst of the **darkness**, (for the mountain did burn with fire,) that ye came near to me, even all the heads of your tribes, and your elders;*

Deuteronomy 5:22-23 WEB, Author's Emphasis

God spoke, and Light with Life instantly entered the waters through the Holy Spirit, changing the visible liquid into living water. The living water is Christ as the light, life, and Word. The Godhead is the source of all life, light and spirit. His Word is the bridge from the invisible to the visible world.

Jesus describes Himself as the "living water" to the Samaritan woman, in John's gospel.

> *Jesus answered her, If you had only known and had recognized God's gift and Who this is that is saying to you, Give Me a drink, you would have asked Him [instead] and **He would have given you living water**.*

> *John 4:10 AMP, Author's Emphasis*

> *She said to Him, Sir, You have nothing to draw with [no drawing bucket] and the well is deep; **how then can You provide living water?** [Where do You get Your living water?]*

> *John 4:11 AMP, Author's Emphasis*

> *He who believes in Me [who cleaves to and trusts in and relies on Me] as the Scripture has said, From his innermost being shall flow [continuously] springs and **rivers of living water**.*

> *John 7:38 AMP, Author's Emphasis*

The woman knew the importance of natural water and she, like Nicodemus, could not understand the reference to living water. Jesus is the master of connecting the visible and invisible worlds together. **Man's responsibility is to recognize his need for spiritual substance outside his physical existence.**

The woman was familiar with religious teaching, but her eyes and ears were spiritually closed because the water she drank was not the "living water." In other words, natural water is essential for physical life, but the "living water" is the only source for spiritual understanding and rebirth.

> *The woman said to Him, I know that Messiah is coming, He Who is called the Christ (the Anointed One); and when He arrives, He will tell us everything we need to know and make it clear to us.*
> *Jesus said to her, I who now speak with you am He.*

> *John 4:25-26 AMP*

This is the sad picture of life in most churches today. There is such little revelation of Christ because so few have tasted the unadulterated "living water." The water offered in most churches today is mixed with additives, which produces religion.

The living water touched everything God created because the very earth was resting "in" Jesus. God formed man from the dust of the earth, which was in the water. The seeds of the earth originated in the living water and remained dormant until the dry land appeared.

Did you ever consider the origin and DNA of all the seeds on the earth? Remember at creation God said, "Light Be." God released His glory impregnating the waters with His DNA and purposes. The dry land appeared, portraying a womb, with the seeds of God under the soil.

41

Then God said, "Let the water under the sky come together in one area, and let the dry land appear." And so it was.

Genesis 1:9 GWD

The Holy Spirit reminded me of the scripture in Isaiah 6:3, which spoke of His Glory filling the whole earth. God's Glory is the DNA of all life and programs all matter perpetually.

Science speaks about energy and matter in relation to one another, but they are unable to explain their origin. I believe the Glory of God is the energy within all life, while matter, on the other hand, is the physical demonstration of His spiritual substance. Therefore, after the dry land, appeared the life of Christ was in all matter including the seeds.

Then God said, Let the earth produce vegetation: plants bearing seeds, each according to its own type, and fruit trees bearing fruit with seeds, each according to its own type. And so it was.

The earth produced vegetation: plants bearing seeds, each according to its own type, and trees bearing fruit with seeds, each according to its own type. God saw that they were good.

There was evening, then morning — a third day.

Genesis 1:11-13 GW

God activated the vegetation the same way He worked the miracles through Jesus.

Have faith that I am in the Father and that the Father is in me: at least, have faith in me because of what I do.

John 14:11 BBE

Everything made by God in the physical realm was through the Holy Spirit and Jesus. The miracle of conversion must be performed in the same manner as creation; otherwise, it will not reproduce the fruit of the Spirit. If God's Glory is not inside the seed, it will not replicate the Godhead.

The DNA of satan and the first Adam corrupted the seeds God planted inside the consciousness of man. Harmful thoughts corrupt the cells of man. Moreover, those same cells affect the thoughts and DNA of the next generations.

Prophetically, right now, water the seeds inside your spirit with the living water which for many of you may have been dormant and lifeless.

Holy Spirit, I ask You to impress those reading to call upon You so they can be reminded of the future planted inside them and their generations. Empower them to uncover and activate those promises of greatness with faith. Lord, I ask You to produce a harvest of reformers from the seeds sown by Your Spirit in this book.

Do you see it? **The model of Genesis is the same today as it was in the beginning.** The life and light is in Him. Adam was formed in the image and likeness of God because He was designed to be God's Son. The ground or dust, contains the very essence of the living water. Our physical body was designed to reflect the living Christ.

God said, Let Us [Father, Son, and Holy Spirit] make mankind in Our image, after Our likeness, and let them have complete authority over the fish of the sea, the birds of the air, the [tame] beasts, and over all of the earth, and over everything that creeps upon the earth.

So God created man in His own image, in the image and likeness of God He created him; male and female He created them.

Genesis 1:26-27 AMP

And the LORD God formed man of the dust of the ground, and breathed into his nostrils the breath of life; and man became a living soul.

Genesis 2:7 WEB

And out of the ground the LORD God formed every beast of the field, and every fowl of the air, and brought them to Adam to see what he would call them; and whatsoever Adam called every living creature, that was its name.

Genesis 2:19 WEB

From Genesis to Revelation the comparison of water with Jesus is unmistakable. Read a few more passages in order for this revelation to empower the seeds in your spirit.

After you see it rise up and shake off the slumber because you are carrying the overcomer's seed. The only thing preventing you from ruling and reigning right now is your wrong thinking.

The voice of the LORD is upon the waters: the God of glory thunders: the LORD is upon many waters.
Psalm 29:3 AMP

His feet glowed like burnished (bright) bronze as it is refined in a furnace, and His voice was like the sound of many waters.
Revelation 1:15 AMP

For the Lamb Who is in the midst of the throne will be their Shepherd, and He will guide them to the springs of the waters of life; and God will wipe away every tear from their eyes.
Revelation 7:17 AMP

THEN HE showed me the river whose waters give life, sparkling like crystal, flowing out from the throne of God and of the Lamb
Revelation 22:1 DAR

Paul sums up the picture we have been drawn at creation with these verses in Colossians.

For by him were all things created, in the heavens and on the earth, things visible and things invisible, whether thrones or dominions or principalities or powers; all things have been created through him, and for him.

He is before all things, and in him all things are held together.

Colossians 1:15-16

Everything resides inside Jesus, both visible and invisible, because without Him nothing has substance or form. He is the reason all things exist and without Him nothing can live.

You are designed to live on the earth and reign in Christ. That is not just a cliché or words from a Christian "life coach," it is the truth and the answer to all of your problems.

Here is what Jesus said to the disciples who would be tortured, stoned and killed and yet they lived in perfect peace.

I have told you these things, so that in Me you may have [perfect] peace and confidence. In the world you have tribulation and trials and distress and frustration; but be of good cheer [take courage; be confident, certain, undaunted] For I have overcome the world. [I have deprived it of power to harm you and have conquered it for you.]

John 16:33 AMP

The world will never understand or support those who are in Christ. Neither will they experience real peace from the visible world. The mind is the greatest obstacle to overcome for someone who wants to understand reality.

The truth exists in Christ who resides in the spiritual and physical realm simultaneously.

CHAPTER 2

ADAM'S
CONSCIOUSNESS

God and His Kingdom represent the only true reality. Faith is the source of His Kingdom, which formed the visible from the invisible world. Man forms his reality from the visible energy and matter, which is a substance of faith.

Therefore, if we call ourselves *born again* Christians we must reside in faith, in order to discern reality. Jesus is the source of faith and in Him is the reality of the visible and invisible.

The mind of the first Adam was deceived and lost its ability to communicate with God. The image and likeness of his creator was lost and resulted in a new identity and consciousness. The visible world became man's reality and resulted in the loss of his spiritual senses. Man depends on his physical senses and corrupted mentality to access reality.

Before we explain the true *born again* experience Jesus described to Nicodemus, lets examine mans condition after Adam's disobedience.

The history of man begins in Adam, but the story of The Kingdom unfolds in Jesus.

The plans of God will never be stopped or changed because it was finished before the foundation of the world. That's right, everything has already been completed and nothing can be added or subtracted from the results.

I realize that whatever God does will last forever. Nothing can be added to it, and nothing can be taken away from it. God does this so that people will fear him.

Whatever has happened (in the past) is present now. Whatever is going to happen (in the future) has already happened (in the past). God will call the past to account.

Ecclesiastes 3: 14-15 GWORD

The thing that has been—it is what will be again, and that which has been done is that which will be done again; and there is nothing new under the sun.

Ecclesiastes 1:9 AMP

The first Adam was created to establish the government of heaven on earth while expanding his consciousness to understand the mind of God. The Father desires a family to share His inner most thoughts and imaginations. The Holy Spirit desires a race of Sons on planet earth whose minds and thoughts are like His own in order to fulfill the Father's dream, "on earth as it is in heaven."

Adam's disobedience on earth was the same treason Lucifer performed in heaven. God's love is not conditional or dependent on angels and man's performance. Adam's unfaithfulness separated man from God and produced sons who loved darkness more than light.

A. DUALITY: BIRTH OF RELIGION

There are many definitions for consciousness, but I believe it is best described as the knowledge, which provides sufficient security to make choices. Humans navigate through life from a "perceived" sense of safety, determined by our beliefs. The right to choose is God's gift to all mankind, but making the right choices requires a "knowing" beyond our perceptions.

Man's current conditions of sickness, disease and fear are the result of choosing to believe a lie. Duality is the fruit of that choice and is responsible for religion. Those who are separated from God live in duality, which is thinking linearly such as, start and finish, right and wrong, good and evil or true and false.

> For **God knows** that in the day you eat it, your eyes will be opened, and you will be like God, knowing good and evil.
>
> *Genesis 3:5 WEB, Author's Empahsis*

The statement above was made by the devil, not God. It is impossible for the devil to "know" what God thinks. Believing the liar or devil forms the consciousness of duality because you are removed from God. Eating the fruit was the act of sin and separated man from The Truth. The nature of sin is the spiritual fruit of iniquity and is passed to every generation.

Man did not understand the laws Moses received from God. They were to convince him of sin and prepare him to be reconciled, not to form a religion. God needed a prophetic bloodline to manifest the second Adam. Unfortunately, man made it a religious model and sustained the system Jesus came to destroy.

Religion will always be the anti-Christ because it is formed from duality and the lie of the devil. **Duality is form without substance.**

> *For [although] they **hold a form** of piety (true religion), they **deny** and reject and are strangers to **the power** of. Avoid [all] such people [turn away from them].*

> *2 Timothy 3:5 AMP, Author's Empahsis*

The consciousness of Adam operates most effectively adhering to religion. Why? Because it provides the false security needed for the sense of "knowing" to choose. The choices from religion reproduce the sin consciousness in each generation.

I believe the Lord is revealing new things for our generation founded on His completed work thousands of years ago.

> *When Jesus had received the sour wine, He said, **It is finished!** And He bowed His head and gave up His spirit.*

> *John 19:30 AMP*

For example one of the biggest lies perpetuated in the evangelical church is that of waiting for Christ to return to do what He finished at the cross.

The Evangelical Church has perpetuated duality among its followers with this view of Bible prophecy. The generally accepted belief is, Christ will return in the clouds and remove His "Bride" in the "rapture" before, during or after a tribulation period on the earth.

Afterwards, Jesus will return again, but this time to earth in order to establish His Kingdom, save the Jews from their enemies and be received as their Messiah. (What makes anyone believe the Jews or any other religious system will receive Jesus today after refusing Him for 2000 years is beyond my comprehension.)

My purpose is not to dispute or agree with this theory, but to identify the form without substance in beliefs of this nature.

> So when they had gathered together, they began to ask him, Lord, **is this the time** when you are restoring the kingdom to Israel?
> He told them, **You are not permitted to know the times** or periods that the Father has set by his own authority.
> But **you will receive power when the Holy Spirit has come upon you,** and you will be my witnesses in Jerusalem, and in all Judea and Samaria, and to the farthest parts of the earth."

> Men of Galilee, why do you stand here looking up into the sky? This same Jesus who has been taken up from you into heaven will come back in the same way you saw him go into heaven."

> Acts 1:7-8,11 NET, Author's Empahsis

The Bible says Jesus will return, but prior to that He tells His disciples they are not permitted to know seasons and times. So is it more important to speculate on His return or to receive the power to overcome by reuniting inside Him?

Ask yourself what the purpose would be for Jesus to die a horrible death 2000 years ago if He had to sit and watch Mankind suffer generation after generation, waiting on His return to do what He already finished?

One purpose of this book is to demonstrate the power from being born "in" Christ. The consciousness of many in Church today, operates in duality because they have the mentality of the first Adam. Attempting to understand the words of Christ requires a spiritual nature, or the rebirth Jesus described to Nicodemus.

I believe the more we focus on our spiritual nature and depend on the Holy Spirit instead of man, the greater authority we will demonstrate throughout the earth. In addition, the Church will recognize the hidden mysteries designed to elevate each generation to a consciousness of overcomers, instead of those waiting to be overcome.

Jesus stripped off His royal robes in Heaven and put on the garments of mortal man to accomplish what Adam failed to do. He defeated the devil, **once and for all** and reestablished His Kingdom, on earth as it is in heaven. He IS (present tense) the eternal Kingdom that reigns, now and forever. The supernatural realms of endless and timeless mysteries are "in Him" and have no beginning or end.

The consciousness of Christ is the "knowing" to make the right choices and power over duality. The devil is still trying to deceive those who have the mind and perceptions of Adam.

The mind of Christ is not a cliché or a new age philosophy, but a living, breathing power, founded on the reality of you in Him and Him in you. Duality ends once you are *born again*.

God's plan is for man to rely on the Holy Spirit the same way Jesus did on earth, not religion or duality. You were born in duality, but through Christ, heaven's door and God's Kingdom are open again. Only this time, satan can never steal it because God Himself established the covenant in His blood.

*But even if our Gospel (the glad tidings) also be hidden (obscured and **covered up with a veil that hinders the knowledge of God**), it is hidden [only] to those who are perishing and obscured [only] to those who are spiritually dying and veiled [only] to those who are lost.*

*For the god of this world has blinded the unbelievers' minds [that they should not discern the truth], preventing them from seeing **the illuminating light** of the Gospel of the glory of Christ (the Messiah), **Who is the Image and Likeness of God.***

2 Corinthians 4:3-4 AMP, Author's Emphasis

The veil of darkness hides the reality of Christ and allows the devil to perform his illusions of duality on mankind. But no more, you have seen the light in the face of Christ from "inside Him."

B. THE ILLUSIONIST

The devil constructs his deceptions from our history of fears and failures, which most people rehearse mentally and verbally. Moreover, he will manifest symptoms in our bodies, which trigger memories of illness of the past. He is in fact, an illusionist and the father of all lies.

His most powerful weapon is access to our memories through our words of fear. People who are afraid often talk about their fears and he records every word.

For example, I recall as a young boy getting sick after being reminded by my mother that playing outside in cold weather, bare footed or without a shirt, would make me sick. I remember audibly rehearsing the memories concerning my last episode of strep throat. Inevitably, in a matter of hours, the symptoms would manifest strep throat. The next thing I knew, my mother would be driving me to the doctor while berating me with the "I told you so" speech. To make matters worse I would be given a shot and a prescription for antibiotics.

The disease manifested as a result of my belief in my mother's warning and the memory of it verbalized internally and externally. My mental image of the physical condition reinforced the cycle of sickness, which I repeated to the very last detail.

This story is to illustrate one of the strategies the devil uses to control us with fear and doubt. Our imaginations and thoughts are fertile fields, but will create a harvest of destruction if fear is added.

Most people make a conscious decision that disease, poverty or disaster will affect their lives and the only choice they are left with, is what or whom they will trust to solve the crisis.

Sadly, most people put their hopes in mans solutions. Will God use a man to resolve our problems? The answer is yes. But He wants us to trust Him first for the solution and not as a last resort. i agree

The prevailing consciousness from the first Adam is the source of our confusion. We must reject every thought formed from fear and unbelief. Those thoughts originate from Adam and are outside of Christ.

> For since by man came death, by man came also
> the resurrection of the dead. For as **in Adam** all die,
> so also in Christ shall all be made alive.

Corinthians 15:21-22 NET, Author's Empahsis

We have been illustrating the difference between being *"in Adam"* versus being *"in Christ"*. The physical world was designed to reflect the spiritual. Choice is ours to make because God is righteous and will not force anyone to love Him. Therefore, God allows satan certain liberties, including deception to provoke man to find his destiny in Christ. i agree

The devil is not creative, but rather predictable. His primary tactic is trickery along with illusions, designed to engage our self-preservation or pride. The illusions most easily believed are constructed from our own selfish nature. Greedy people believe lies, which makes the devils job easier.

For example, many people fall victims to "get rich quick" schemes because their sin consciousness convinces them they are immune from being deceived. We have all sinned and lying is at the top of the list.

The truth is, the devil has legal right to those who reside in Adam and have lied or cheated others. Those who have lied will reap the same. The illusionist is skilled at making one believe a lie because he is the father of all lies. So, if we are "in Christ," who is The Truth we would not be deceived.

Even our idea of self is composed from a false illusion conceived by the mind's images of reality. Those unreal concepts and pictures are the foundation for the devil's illusionary tricks.

Illusions are easily perpetuated on those who are preoccupied with their own self-image and identity. Fame, popularity and notoriety are more desirable to those whose minds are engaged with the illusion of self.

The illusion the devil uses to trap people originates from the images acted out and spoken. The young form their self-images from movies, games and peers. They are inundated with advertisements and commercials designed to influence their desires and self-images.

The world of video or cinema is closely related to mental thoughts and imaginations. As a result, it is not difficult to use subconscious imagery as a form of self-hypnosis against those who are searching for an identity. It is easy to understand why the youth of today are attracted to the world of video games. Reality is blurred on the screens of monitors and becomes an easy transition from the video screen to the mind.

Rejection is one of the fears the devil uses on the younger generation, along with unforgiveness, which drives them to act out abhorrent behaviors.

The corruption of the human mind is the number one goal of the devil and his demons. Illusions are convincing to those whose minds are conditioned by this world's ideas and images of reality.

The spiritual realm is less important or relevant to those whose minds are continually evaluating the latest fashions and video games. Their search for God becomes critical only after a crisis or bad report. Then after all physical options are exhausted people turn to God.

> *I will not leave you all alone. I will come back to you. In a little while the world will no longer see me, but you will see me. You will live because I live.*
> *John 14:18-19 GW*

Jesus is explaining the transition to reality from the physical world. Reality is the true life outside the physical world. It is visible to those who have made the transition into Christ.

The mind of Adam is rarely at rest. It is nurtured and stimulated by "fear," which is the catalyst in thoughts nourishing sin, sickness and death.

Most people who experience physical discomfort or symptoms of sickness and the like quickly assume the worst even if they profess hope and faith. Society and the majority of church members are conditioned to accept and trust the doctor's report as the final word in diagnoses and treatment, even if they profess differently.

The act of believing a symptom requires our imaginations and pride. Imagination accesses the picture from our minds and pride manifests the symptoms. Most people faced with physical discomfort or symptoms will make a self-diagnoses based on "worse case scenarios."

The majority of people would rather be self-fulfilling prophets at their own expense. The same energy to believe in the cross and the price paid for our healing is spent to believe a bad report.

In other words, people often times manifest the disease they predict, in order to proclaim, "I told you so" and identify with the majority of suffering humanity.

Those with a bad medical diagnosis, such as cancer, are presented with a choice of either trusting another person's illusion or believing the promise of The One who overcame all things. More often than not, those with such a diagnosis believe the physicians. *i agree its true*

Once a transition is made from thinking and talking about the disease to actually picturing it in the body, the next step is inevitable. The symptoms will appear worse and depending on the level of fear the outcome will not be good.

I believe more faith is released from people at the solutions offered by physicians than the words of Christ. Does God use science to solve our problems? The answer is yes.

God uses doctors to help unbelievers and immature Christians, but His solution for all diseases hung on a cross 2000 years ago. In Christ, there are no diseases and divine health is the life of those who manifest His Kingdom. *amen me*

For you died, and your life is hidden with Christ in God

Colossians 3:3 BBE

It is necessary to understand the reality of Adam, which is the preoccupation with self. Science has proven man is conscious of his environment ten seconds out of every minute. **In other words, fifty seconds of each minute the "self" is consumed with its perceptions and needs.**

C. ADAM'S IMAGE AND LIKENESS

Adam's original image and likeness was replaced with sin, which perpetually corrupts man's spiritual DNA. Moreover, sin creates the void in man's identity he attempts to fill from the world of illusion.

Science has made astonishing discoveries, which demonstrate the vacuum we are born into and the preoccupation of each generation to discover the real "self."

We use sentences everyday describing ourselves as "I", but have you ever thought about the actual location inside your body of the person you identify as "I?"

According to science, there is not a "physical" place inside your body where "you" actually exist. We are made of atoms, which are made from particles and waves spinning at lightening speed in space. So what is an atom?

Atoms are the basic building blocks of "stuff" we call matter, which make up objects. A table, chair, air, even you are made up of atoms. Atoms are invisible to the naked eye. There are about 20 million hydrogen atoms on the head of a straight pin.

Science believes the universe, also made of atoms, is empty and what we have always thought to be solid is actually an illusion. Early physicists, such as Einstein, describe our belief of solidity as illusionary and unreal according their scientific data.

If a single atom were enlarged to the size of a football field the solid part of its nuclei could be compared to a grain of rice and the rest would be empty. The nucleus of the atom accounts for 99.99% of all of its entire matter and mass making the atom almost entirely comprised of empty.

Atoms form the structure of the physical world and are mostly void. Nevertheless, we perceive the world and our human bodies to be solid. According to science that perception is made from a person we identify as "I," who is an illusion of our senses and resides in empty space.

If we had the proper microscopes we could see the world of things we identify as solid, vibrating at speeds equal to their molecular makeup. Wood, glass, metal and brick all vibrate at different frequencies because of their physical composition or atoms.

Atoms can be described as energy vibrating at different frequencies. They form various shapes and densities of matter relative to their speeds. **Everything is moving faster than our eyes can see and creates the illusion of solid.**

To illustrate this principle, think of an airplane propeller spinning at high speeds on the wing of a plane. If you have ever noticed it appears to be a solid object whirling around instead of individual blades.

Our five senses have pictured the body to be solid, even though scientifically, we are made up of 99.99% empty space. For a parent, that explains a great deal when trying to feed growing teenagers. The most important principle to understand is that everything is moving or vibrating at different speeds, even the "person" you identify as yourself.

Moreover, science describes electromagnetic fields in relation to each person's atomic structures. In other words, thoughts create an electromagnetic field, which attracts energy and matter relative to their speed. Therefore, those who want to attract heaven must vibrate at its speed. For me, this is accomplished in worship.

On the other hand, people who are fearful and afraid attract circumstances and people with a similar frequency or vibration. The power of thought is magnified with spoken words. **Our thoughts attract energy and words draw matter.**

The same principals are at work in the spiritual dimensions. The thoughts of Christ vibrate at frequencies outside the realm of time and space and attract heaven's glory. Heavens power to affect our life is limited by our consciousness of Christ.

The origin of our thoughts is the subject of many books and discussions, but I believe thoughts are formed from spiritual influences, which result in our consciousness. We are spiritual beings with invisible antennas attracting the energy we are unconsciously transmitting.

The Holy Spirit never stops sending us His transmissions of love and acceptance from the Father. One reason we do not receive His communication is because of the noise we produce. The minds unrest in attempting to find an image or likeness to portray generates racket or feedback.

The never-ending search to find a physical purpose or identity prevents us from hearing the voice of Jesus singing our names and describing our destiny. The sound of His voice has been described as many waters making it easy to resonate within our bodies, which are primarily composed of water.

Those whose minds are fixed on Christ will be led by the Holy Spirit, while those who are captivated by this world, will be influenced by the prince of the power of the air. Most scientists portray the visible world as illusionary, because matter is formed from atoms, which are predominately empty space. The world in reality is the way it was in the beginning described in Genesis, void. Jesus has given us the authority to create heaven on earth in the same manner as He did in the beginning. Reread the last sentence again and let it penetrate your spirit.

Everyday we are presented with the opportunity to eat from the tree of life or from the knowledge of good and evil the same as the first Adam. The choice to live inside Christ and His Kingdom or to live in the world of the knowledge of good and evil, right or wrong, true or false is ours to choose.

Religion, philosophy and science are not the solution for mankind, and in fact, they are the problem. Jesus illustrated the model and provided the resource through the Holy Spirit.

The mind of man is designed to transform the physical realm by using the spiritual. Adam lost that ability through sin, but Jesus with the Holy Spirit, has opened the portals of heaven again for man's access. The way is easy to understand, but submission is difficult.

The nature of sin has not only corrupted the mind of man, but has infected the body as well. Man is a triune being, which simply means, he is a spirit with a soul and resides in a temporal body. Man is designed to house the Godhead, and reproduce Sons of God throughout the earth.

satan's plan is to destroy man's mind and eventually kill the body. The devil combines fear and illusion to produce unhealthy cravings and preoccupy his thoughts, resulting in sickness and disease.

Follow along, as we uncover the strategy the devil uses to destroy our soul and body. God wants to arm you with sufficient knowledge to break the strongholds and addictions you felt helpless to overcome. The Lord has heard your cry and today is your day of salvation over sickness and disease.

D. THE CHEMICAL ADAM

God formed Adam from the earth and simultaneously ignited his soul and spirit with His breath. Adam was spiritually connected on heavens respirator system through God's breath, thoughts and blood. As long as he was joined with God, sin could not destroy the soul or body. Sin destroys the mind first and eventually the body will develop physical diseases.

Thoughts are the source of sin and our blood is the medium for destruction.

This section will illustrate the destructive path of sin, beginning first with the mind and finishing in the body.

Physiologically our brains are made of tiny nerve cells called neurons. These neurons have tiny, "hair-like" fibers, which connect with other neurons to form a network. Thoughts and memories are produced in each place the nerve endings attach. These connections form a "mental library" of experiences and relationships, which becomes the minds resource center.

That means, over time, all of our ideas, desires, imaginations, thoughts and feelings construct an integrated network of sensations throughout the brain and central nervous system of the body. These highways of experiences construct elaborate associations with our emotions.

For example, if one thinks about a certain relationship, such as friendship, it might elicit a memory of pain linked to hurt, which may be connected to anger or revenge, which in turn evokes the image of a specific person or event, returning to that person's concept of friendships.
Suppose Diana falls in love with John and marries him. She discovers John to be unfaithful and is emotionally devastated. The pain she feels becomes hurt and anger, which may evolve into revenge and suspicion towards all men. She divorces John and builds an emotional wall of victimization formed from the sensations of hurt, pain, anger and suspicion.

The wall of emotions is constructed from the neuro net or "mental library" and sophisticatedly joined throughout the central nervous system to thoughts associated with love or marriage. The pain from the relationship will be reinforced by these images and concepts, each time she identifies herself as a victim.

These "movies" we watch inside our minds happen instantaneously and are the perceived realities, which activate our emotions. The brain is unable to distinguish between images outside the mind from those on the inside. All of the mind's pictures are first formed behind the cerebral cortex with light and sound from our eyes and ears.

No one is capable of making objective observations in the present because of past experiences and our current emotional condition. Each time we experience a new relationship or situation, we measure it with past memories. This prevents anyone from being objective consequently all of our observations are subjective.

All of our stored experiences from the past contaminate the present and adds further emotional weight to the images we define as "Me." The phrase, "living in the past" is true and it is one of the hinderances to our faith.

In essence, our perceptions of reality are made from our "mirror" of memories. It is this reflection, which contributes to the personalities of who we believe ourselves to be. In most cases, the life you are living is almost entirely a reflection of past experiences.

The mind forms digital memories through the fives senses aided primarily with light and sound. That means even touching, tasting or smelling a physical object is compared with the past digital images stored in the mind's library.

Are you beginning to understand the relationship illusions play in our perceptions of reality, particularly as it pertains to light and sound?

Our pictures of reality produce emotions from thoughts and images connected to our nerve network in the brain's frontal lobe. We have determined our senses to be unreliable and therefore, incapable of discerning reality. But that does not prevent persons from attaching their emotional lives to these false images, which ultimately produces bad attitudes and behaviors.

For example, if we are consistently angry, sad or depressed, the respective link, which is formed in the neuro network, becomes more integrated and harder to change. We eventually form a destructive long-term relationship with those emotions. The network expands and increases in more harmful behaviors the more we respond to the feelings.

On the other hand, by laughing or singing one can break connections formed in our neuro nets. These activities can excite nerve cells that serve to interrupt thoughts and break patterns of destructive behavior.

Desire is the most addictive emotion in our bodies and it is most often displayed with pictures and images. The images or imaginations are chemical sensations stored in the minds frontal lobe.
If we perceive the illusions of our thoughts to be reality, the body will shape its emotions around those beliefs. Those beliefs will create an imbalance in the body's emotional center and activates a gland called the Hypothalamus.

Our brains are the greatest pharmaceutical factories on the planet. One of the responsibilities of the Hypothalamus Gland is to assemble chemicals most closely associated with our emotional cravings. These chemicals are called peptides, which are types of amino acids.

The hypothalamus secretes chemical compounds that closely match the emotions. There are chemicals for sadness, anger, victimization, lust, depression and joy, for example.

If our brains or bodies encounter any of those emotions, the hypothalamus will manufacture a peptide to offset those feelings. It then releases those peptides through our blood stream where it enters the cells.

Picture an envelope delivered to a mailbox and inside the envelope is a letter with coded information designed to balance the cells condition. Peptides are very strong amino acids whose main function is to balance the emotional center of the organism.

Neurologists have identified a peptide called enkephalins, which is known to act as a bonding agent in opiates, such as heroin and morphine. This natural occurring peptide is released in our blood streams during a response to self- destructive stress. The mind will manufacture and release these peptides in attempt to sedate the central nervous system and prevent death.

The body's cells are designed to regenerate most effectively when the chemicals or amino acids are alkaline. Thoughts of happiness, peace and joy create the proper nutrition for healthy cell reproduction. On the other hand, sadness, anger, rage, jealousy, and depression produce acidic chemicals, which change the cells DNA structure and character.

In essence, our emotions trigger images, which produce substances, which can alter our cells. The cells form addictions to the chemicals and long-term relationships with the emotions. The body reflects the chemical it demands most often.

Consuming pharmaceutical drugs weakens and eventually destroys the body's immune system. Over time, the body looses its ability to produce proper chemicals to protect its organs.

i agree

The body makes demands on the hypothalamus to supply chemicals, to match the emotions of betrayal, paranoia, physical and sexual appetites or the like. The mind does not judge the character of the person making the demand. It simply supplies the chemicals to satisfy the emotional trauma created from the first Adam's sin nature. Unless the character changes, the body and mind will be slaves to the emotions.

We can become addicted to the chemicals our body creates even if the behaviors are destructive. For example, people who view themselves as victims will invent scenarios in their mind, which eventually attract a "real life" situation, in order to produce the amino acid.

The more convinced we are of the reality from our emotions the more addicted we become to the feelings from our mind's pharmaceutical factory. Thus, our bodies become the center for decisions instead of our mind. The mind is the "drug dealer" supplying the chemicals and memories to support our addictions. Our bodies, at this point, control our appetites physically and mentally.

A person who is habitually depressed deforms the cells and inhibits the reception of the natural amino acids. The body will reflect the diseased cells in physical appearances such as wrinkles, dark circles around the eyes and stooped shoulders.

After a period of time, the cells can become agitated and transmit images of desperation to the brain. This is the first signs of addiction and will resemble a cinema presentation complete with pictures and narration. **The star of the movie is you and the plot is constructed from the emotions craving your attention**. Images such as depression, anger or victimization are played over and over inside the minds of those addicted to these feelings.

For example, persons with eating disorders will hear voices inside their heads screaming, "feed me," "I'm starving," or "if I don't get food now I'll die." These voices are complete with pictures displaying large plates of their favorite foods along with memories of when they felt completely satisfied. The pictures associated with the sound are very hard addictions to break.

One of the most common amino acids scientists have identified is Ghrelin, which tells the brain its time to eat. When the "voices" of addiction tells the brain it is hungry, the hypothalamus will manufacture Ghrelin in an effort to satisfy the hunger and silence the voices.

Unfortunately, if the cells have been deformed from abuse of the amino acid, the body will not "feel" satisfied and continue to eat. In addition, demonic activity will always be at the root of addiction, it is not just physiological.

Eating refined sugar creates an imbalance in the pancreas because it raises the insulin levels, usually resulting in diabetes. The craving for this type of sugar is akin to drug addiction. The body forms an attachment to the insulin "rush," which temporarily makes one feel good.

Those who abuse white sugar will develop diabetes and doctors will prescribe insulin resulting most often in side effects from blindness to limb loss. Consequently, eating sugar or craving anything harmful to ones body will lead to destructive diseases.

This is an important principle to understand. If you feel helpless to control destructive desires you most likely are under demonic influence and require deliverance. The Holy Spirit has used me to deliver those from addictions created from demonic influences.

A way to break behaviors is to change the images stored in the mind. One function of the mind is to protect the body with proper nutritional desires. However, if emotions control ones thoughts and images, the brain will produce peptides or amino acids to satisfy a crisis.

Often times, people from unhappy relationships desire the sensations and feelings they once experienced before the separation or divorce. In most cases, persons attempt to relive the sensations or feelings associated with love in future companions. In essence, they are addicted to the expectations or preconceived ideas of "being in love."

Those connections were formed from the chemical reactions their emotions demanded in the past. The results of future companionships are usually predictable because of the instability of all addictions. People "fall" in and out of love because addictive personalities need stronger and stronger drugs to satisfy their cravings.

Most persons become physically weak and exhausted from the emotional rollercoaster produced from chemical addictions the body demands for its emotional "fix." That is why it is so hard to quiet the mind.

After the body is unable to supply the chemicals needed, people will often turn to physicians to prescribe stronger synthetic medications. The synthetic drugs create a more serious imbalance also resulting in side effects. If you have ever watched drug commercials describing their side effects, you will know this to be true. *true*

Furthermore, the cells become so deformed that even if we exercise and feed the body with proper nutrition and vitamins, our cells are unable to process the healthy nutrients.

Perceiving reality with our five senses is dangerous enough, but if our senses are emotionally damaged, our view of life is forever altered. We will be a slave to our emotions and chemically addicted.

In summary, the body is made of billions of cells whose primary purpose is to protect the body and reproduce healthy cells. The peptides or amino acids are designed to balance the system. The cell has been called the smallest conscious unit in the body.

In my opinion, the cells are God's divine energy inside our complex machines. The cells are indeed conscious and if our thoughts are connected to Christ, we can experience divine health. *i agree*

The Bible says The Kingdom of God is not eating and drinking, but righteousness, peace and joy in the Holy Spirit. That alone is a recipe for divine health in our body and soul. *Amen!*

CHAPTER 3

THE SECOND ADAM

The greatest desire of God is for men to discover Him as the righteousness, peace and joy they are seeking. The Kingdom of heaven was established on earth through Jesus to satisfy the heart of His Father. God's Kingdom is visible to those who are born in Christ, but it is invisible to those who remain in Adam.

Religion has constructed doctrines and theology describing the *born again* experience. Jesus is both the visible and invisible manifestation of that birth. He was born from a virgin by the Spirit and is also the "water" He describes to Nicodemus.

A. YOU MUST BE *BORN AGAIN*

Those from evangelical churches have heard the phrase *born again* followed by the description on "how" to receive the experience. But, even after reciting the "sinners prayer," my life was more or less, unaffected.

Several years later, I discovered the experience to be much more than repeating scriptures after a pastor or joining a church. I realized my mental condition, which was the result of Adam, prevented my spiritual birth into Christ and was why

Jesus said, "repent." It was that revelation which provoked my repentance and hunger to do whatever it took to experience a true birth "into" Christ.

The *born again* experience taught by most churches is obviously not transforming people or society would be radically different. Churches are experiencing growth, but the same sins exist inside the four walls as they do outside. Moreover, the parishioners are sick and diseased and in many cases, worse off than those who have no church affiliation.

There are some whose lives have been changed and are making a real difference for Christ wherever they go. But for the most part, those in churches form their opinions and beliefs from popular opinion and accepted world views.

We have spoken about the parallel between creation and being *born again*, but I believe this should be explained in such a way that no one will misunderstand the power in this transformation.

This is not a philosophical journey one can experience with a mind, which has not renounced the structures of the first Adam. That is why the message Jesus preached was "repent," or change the way you think.

The transformation of the mind begins with the recognition of ones condition and the passion to repent. **In order for a human being to see the Kingdom of God, one must be birthed from a dimension outside of time**.

The following conversation between Nicodemus and Jesus has a greater significance if we apply our understanding of water and Spirit.

Now there was a Pharisee named Nicodemus, a leader of the Jews.

He came to Jesus by night and said to him, Rabbi, we know that you are a teacher who has come from God; for no one can do these signs that you do apart from the presence of God.

Jesus answered him, Very truly, I tell you, no one can see the kingdom of God without being born from above

Nicodemus said to him, "How can anyone be born after having grown old? Can one enter a second time into the mother's womb and be born?

Matthew 3:1-4 NRSV

Jesus answered the question Nicodemus never asked. Nicodemus is amazed with the signs and wonders and Jesus tells him why he is not doing the same. Paraphrasing, Nicodemus you are Jew by birth, but not a citizen of God's Kingdom.

Jesus answered, "Truly, truly, I say to you, unless one is born of water and the Spirit, he cannot enter into the kingdom of God.

John 3:5 NASB

I believe the real *born again* experience is achieved the way Jesus was physically birthed.

And the angel answered and said to her, "The Holy Spirit will come upon you, and the power of the Most High will overshadow you; and for that reason the holy offspring shall be called the Son of God.

Luke 1:35 NASB

The Holy Spirit impregnated Mary with Jesus to preserve the bloodline from His Father and reestablish His Kingdom. The model is still the same, only now Jesus is the womb, not Mary.

Jesus births those who have been impregnated by the water and Spirit into The Christ or Kingdom of God.

Long ago, when God made covenant with Abraham, He did more than make him a father. God opened the physical womb of Sarah and the spiritual womb of Israel. I am speaking of the redeemed nation from Abraham's loins. **He protected that womb throughout history until the "author" of the prophetic words became the Living Word.**

Our spirits are awakened through the impregnation of the Holy Ghost. The womb is Jesus and the birth culminates in Christ consciousness. **The Kingdom of God, although invisible to the natural mind, transforms reality from the senses to faith.**

The spiritual rebirth is not a scriptural recital so often practiced at the altars of most churches and seen on Christian television. It is a transformation demonstrated by the revelation of the unseen realm.

In other words, those who have been birthed into The Kingdom of heaven actually witness heaven. I have had many encounters with angelic beings whose purpose was to assist me in establishing God's Kingdom.

On a number of occasions, angels have accompanied me into heaven to orchestrate worship and warfare for specific assignments. Angels are heaven's enforcers of salvation and we are the Holy Spirits prophetic mouthpieces on earth.

> *Are they not all helping spirits, who are sent out as servants to those whose heritage will be salvation?*

> *Hebrews 1:14 BBE*

Jesus says to seek first the Kingdom of heaven, which is who He Is. The Kingdom of Heaven is not a physical place, but the **mind** of Christ.

Jesus gives us more insight into The Kingdom of God and man's kingdom conversion in the following scriptures.

> *That which has birth from the flesh is flesh, and that which has birth from the Spirit is spirit.*

> *Do not be surprised that I say to you, It is necessary for you to have a second birth*

> *John 3:6-7 BBE*

It is necessary for Jesus to further distinguish the character and nature of persons born of flesh from those born of The Spirit.

What the modern day church labels as "carnal Christians," are not born of the water and Spirit. **They have knowledge, but their minds are still connected to Adam preventing them from being impregnated by the Holy Spirit.** Paul makes a statement in Corinthians that I believe proves my point:

> *Brothers and sisters, I couldn't talk to you as spiritual people but as people still influenced by your corrupt nature. You were infants in your faith in Christ.*

Corinthians 3:1

Jesus purchased all men through the cross. All men belong to Him, but all men are not citizens of God's Kingdom nor saved. Only birth by The Water and The Spirit will make them citizens of the Kingdom of God.

B. SCRIPTURAL MODEL

It is important to revisit the conversation between Jesus and a Samaritan woman. Open your spirits as you read the dialogue between a religious person and Jesus the "spiritual womb" of God.

> *The Samaritan woman said to him, How is it that you, a Jew, ask a drink of me, a woman of Samaria? (Jews do not share things in common with Samaritans.)*

> *Jesus answered her, If you knew the gift of God, and who it is that is saying to you, Give me a drink, you would have asked him, and he would have given you living water.*

The woman said to him, Sir, you have no bucket, and the well is deep. Where do you get that living water?

Are you greater than our ancestor Jacob, who gave us the well, and with his sons and his flocks drank from it?

Jesus said to her, everyone who drinks of this water will be thirsty again, but those who drink of the water that I will give them will never be thirsty. The water that I will give will become in them a spring of water gushing up to eternal life.

The woman said to him, Sir, give me this water, so that I may never be thirsty or have to keep coming here to draw water.

John 4:9-15 NRSV

This conversation illustrates the mind of the first Adam attempting to understand the spiritual world. Jesus begins the conversation by asking for natural water.

Obviously, He was physically thirsty and hungry because the disciples went to find food, as mentioned in the scripture. Moreover, you will notice after reading the entire chapter, Jesus never drinks or eats. This ministers to me because the Holy Spirit has sustained me with spiritual food and water on a number of occasions.

The mind of the first Adam is unaccustomed to the realm of the spirit and terms such as "living water." The woman tells

Jesus she wants the "water" so she will not be thirsty or work drawing water any longer.

In other words, (paraphrasing) give me what will improve my life without forcing me to change my behavior.

Unfortunately, the majority of those who identify themselves as *born again* are in that condition. Furthermore, most Christian churches across the world do not know how to change their followers.

The natural mind is unable to understand the "new birth" or the Kingdom of God. The "kingdom" message is popular in many churches, but it has become more of a buzzword than a true transformation for society and religious settings.

Notice Jesus asks her to do something that will eventually lead her to a spiritual encounter.

> *"Go, call your husband, and come back." The woman answered him, "I have no husband." Jesus said to her, "You are right in saying, 'I have no husband'; for you have had five husbands, and the one you have now is not your husband. What you have said is true!" The woman said to him, "Sir, I see that you are a prophet.*
>
> *John 4:16-19*

The Samaritan woman identified Jesus as a prophet because He knew her marital situation and religious training. Jesus is "The" prophet because the nature of a true prophet is to constantly see heaven and always establish on earth what is in heaven.

Another purpose of the prophet is to minister living water to those dying of spiritual thirst. In other words, a prophet should be perpetually gushing with fresh water or revelations of Christ not necessarily "giving a word" to those who do not want to drink from Jesus.

The water that I will give will become in them a spring of water gushing up to eternal life.

John 4:14b NRSV

Religion is the same today as it was 2000 years ago. Religion destroys the prophets because fresh revelations of Christ undermine those who desire to control people with fear and lies. Jesus came to fulfill the law and reestablish The Kingdom.

Our forefathers worshipped on this mountain, but you Jews say that the place where people must worship is in Jerusalem.

Believe me, said Jesus, the time is coming when you will worship the Father neither on this mountain nor in Jerusalem.

You worship One of whom you know nothing. We worship One whom we know; for salvation comes from the Jews.

But a time is coming—no, has already come—when the true worshippers will worship the Father with true spiritual worship; for indeed the Father desires such worshippers.

God is Spirit; and those who worship Him must bring Him true spiritual worship.

I know, replied the woman, that Messiah is coming—the Christ, as He is called. When He has come, He will tell us everything.

I am He, said Jesus — I who am now talking to you.

John 4:20-26 WEY

The conversation between the woman and Jesus centers around theology of what will happen in the future versus entering The Kingdom of God now.

The woman believes as most of the modern day church, in order to have overcoming power Jesus must return. This lie has paralyzed the church from assuming her role as the authority in the earth. Jesus says NOW IS the time for the overcoming power to be realized and exercised. The living water is the entrance into The Kingdom of God.

The conversation Jesus has with a blind man after he is healed also demonstrates the church mindset today. He was a religious Jew waiting on the Messiah to deliver him from all his problems.

Do you believe in the Son of Man? He answered and said, And who is He, Lord, that I may believe in Him. Jesus said to him, You have both seen Him, and He is the one who is talking with you.". And he said, Lord, I believe." And he worshiped Him.

John 9:35-38 NASB

Drinking "The living water" awakens the spirit and the immediate response is to worship the One who gives us life. Worship opens heaven and allows us to see The Kingdom of heaven.

The Bible says grace and truth came by Jesus (*John 1:17*). There is no way one can worship the Father who is Spirit, without drinking the living water, who is Jesus. The power to transform your life lies in your thirst for The Truth.

It seems the majority of those who call themselves *born again* are waiting on Jesus to finish what has been done. The same happened in His time as it does today. Religion waits, while The Kingdom advances. What are you doing?

C. ENTERING HIM IS *BORN AGAIN*

Religion makes people "stiff necked" and resistant to change. The majority of those in North American churches are content with messages of self-improvement and prosperity. Many see no reason to concern themselves with messages or ministries which challenge their status quo.

I became a Christian in my early teens and my life reflected the same attitude as those before me. I eventually realized my beliefs were founded on someone else's experience.

In other words, my recitation of the "sinners prayer" and baptism was an empty formula that had not produced anything in my "nature" other than a religious facade. I was sick, depressed, broke and struggling with the same desires as those who never darkened the doors of a church.

83

The time had come to make a life choice from a personal knowledge and experience, rather than a pastor or preacher. I locked myself in my room and sincerely cried out to know Him. The Holy Spirit responded to my sincerity. His love and gentleness melted my heart and illuminated my mind.

The scriptures became the living word revealing the mysteries of The Kingdom. The light and life of Christ penetrated my soul as if Jesus Himself were standing in front of me. Jesus became the lover of my soul and I gladly gave Him my life. He did not ask me to die for Him. I felt as if I was already dead to this world. It was during that time Jesus taught me what I am about to show those of you willing to change.

He said, *"My people are choosing to perish for lack of knowledge because I have been sharing this message for generations. It has grieved My Spirit to see the countless thousands refusal to enter the spiritual dimension. Those who will make the effort to change will be rewarded in this life and in the ages to come, everlasting life."*

Those of you who have ears to hear and eyes to see I will show you what the Holy Spirit revealed to me. Pay close attention to the phrase "in Me."

*But if I am doing them, then have belief in the works even if you have no belief **in me**; so that you may see clearly and be certain that the **Father is in me and I am in the Father.***

John 10:38 BBE

*I am the vine, you are the branches: he who is **in me** at all times as I am **in him**, gives much fruit, because without me you are able to do nothing.*

*If a man does not keep himself **in me**, he becomes dead and is cut off like a dry branch; such branches are taken up and put in the fire and burned.*

*If you are **in me** at all times, and my words are **in you**, then anything for which you make a request will be done for you.*

John 15:5-7 BBE

*May they all be one! Even as you, Father, are **in me and I am in you**, so let them be in us, so that all men may come to have faith that you sent me.*

John 17:21 BBE

I in them, and you in me, *so that they may be made completely one, and so that it may become clear to all men that you have sent me and that they are loved by you as I am loved by you.*

John 17:23 BBE

It should be obvious at this point the power to transform ones thoughts is achieved through entering Christ. One of the best scriptures to demonstrate the power and reality of this statement is below.

Don't you believe that I am in the Father and the Father is in me? What I'm telling you doesn't come from me. The Father, who lives in me, does what he wants.

Believe me when I say that I am in the Father and that the Father is in me. Otherwise, believe me because of the things I do.

"I can guarantee this truth: Those who believe in me will do the things that I am doing. They will do even greater things because I am going to the Father.

John 14:10-12 GW

The words Jesus speaks are spirit and life because He is speaking only what the Father speaks through Him. The model of transformation and genuine authority to alter circumstances lies in these verses.

Jesus said, if you want to do the same and greater works, you would need to believe "in me." The religious person reads that verse and interprets it to mean something entirely different.

Jesus just described the relationship He has with His Father. We must assume, in order to perform greater works, one must follow the same model. Therefore, the believer must reside "in Jesus" the same way He is in the Father.

In other words, each time we read scripture that says, "believe in me" we should interpret it to mean, "BELIEVE, FROM WITHIN ME."

On that day you will know that I am in my Father and that you are in me and that I am in you.

John 14:20 GW

The proof of the real transition is "on that day." What day is He speaking about? Is it the rapture or the day of His return? NO! It is the day those who profess to be *born again* perform miracles equal to or greater than Him. That is the day, Jesus said you would know He is in the Father and you are IN HIM.

Those who do not make that transition are not *born again.* Furthermore, their lives will be no different from those who profess any other philosophy. **Philosophy is a mental belief not a spiritual transformation.** Jesus is the spiritual transition into the power of the creative God.

The majority of confusion evolves from the interpretation of verses, which describe a belief or faith "in" Jesus or His name. Instead of the model Jesus so clearly states in John 14:10-11. It seems to imply we can know Him the same way people know the president of their country. They know his name and have probably even seen his face on television, but they have not personally met in most cases.

For example, many people may believe in a politician they support. But if that politician fixes a personal problem for you because of his position, your belief will change to trust. **Trust is formed as a result of intimate knowledge and experience about the person.**

Faith is the byproduct of trust and is the result of living "in Christ." Those who "say they believe" in Jesus Christ are, for the most part, depending on someone else's experience of

87

Christ. That was my problem after thinking I was a *born again* Christian. I did not posses enough faith to stop a headache.

> *To make their eyes open, turning them from the dark to the light, and from the power of satan to God, so that they may have forgiveness of sins and a heritage among those **who are made holy by faith in me***.

Acts 26:18 BBE

I recall responding to an invitation in a church to accept Jesus Christ as my Lord by coming to the front altar. I repeated some verses after the pastor and was told I was *born again*. I was given some literature and encouraged to join the church and be baptized, which I did.

I was taught salvation and repeated the verses found in *Romans 10:9-10* and *Ephesians 2:8-9*. The verses are in the Bible and part of the truth. Jesus is the complete truth and after I experienced Him by the Holy Spirit, my belief changed to faith. **Faith will always grow proportionate to ones personal loss of identity.**

"Entering Christ," I found is achieved only after my spirit connects back to The Spirit and regains dominion over the soul. The soul was my master and until I surrendered control by sacrificing my ego, entering Him was not possible.

The spirit is also where faith resides. The reason I had such little faith was because my soul was in charge.

> *He who has faith and is given baptism will get salvation; but he who has not faith will be judged.*

88

And these signs will be with those who have faith: in my name they will send out evil spirits; and they will make use of new languages;

They will take up snakes, and if there is poison in their drink, it will do them no evil; they will put their hands on those who are ill, and they will get well.

Mark 16:16-18 BBE

There is no shortcut to enter Christ and His Kingdom. It all begins at the cross, but it does not end there. Today's church must assume their responsibility in solving the problems of society.

Jesus destroyed the works of the devil with the power of God. He said the works I do are not mine but Gods. That is our model and if our desire is to be like Him, we will stop being religious and call upon the Lord until we are changed.

Kingdom conversion is entering into Christ by drinking the living water through the Spirit. How do you drink spiritual water? I can tell you my experience, but it is not a formula or by any means the only way.

C. MY CONVERSION

Religion and other people's opinions had made me so weary, I closed myself off from everyone and everything and just began to cry out for the truth. Between my tears and confessions of wrong thinking and acting, something happened.

One way to describe the experience was that my mind was being immersed inside peace and joy, which it could not understand or comprehend.

Suddenly, I felt a refreshing of my soul that felt like my whole being was being washed from the inside out.

I experienced an inner "knowing" of having entered a "new" life with an invisible energy that had personality and love without words.

Hence, no words can describe the overwhelming love and sense of belonging I experienced. The power was awesome and terrifying at the same time. Frightening because I felt vulnerable in the presence of God's holiness, making me afraid of thinking or doing anything that would offend Him.

All I did was worship Him with all my being. Everything in me cried out Holy, Holy, Holy.

My life was changed, I had tasted the living water and been invited into His Kingdom. This is not the end of my conversion, only a snap shot of the beginning of a never-ending pursuit to "know" Him.

I recalled Jesus asking the Samaritan woman a question, He said:

> *If you had knowledge of what God gives freely and who it is who says to you, Give me water, you would make your prayer to him, and he would give you living water.*
>
> *John 4:10 BBE*

The truth will only set you free if you know Him who is the truth. Jesus makes it a point to tell the woman that you are worshipping what you do not know.

You give worship, but without knowledge of what you are worshipping, we give worship to what we have knowledge of:

John 4:22 BBE

This is and has been one of the problems throughout time. People may have religious knowledge about Jesus, but very few have the knowledge Jesus was describing. He is talking about the pearl or the treasure, which motivates you to sell everything you have. That is the living water He offers to those with knowledge of who He is and what He is worth.

Are you getting thirsty? Drinking Jesus produces power because He is the living water that springs up into eternal life.

My life changed dramatically after I became thirsty for something more than a mental knowledge of Jesus. Worship was all I wanted to do. I did not care what others thought or how I appeared.

All I cared about was making it known on earth and in heaven that Jesus was the center of my attention. He was the one I wanted to please and if that meant dancing in front of people to express my love, that's what I did.

There is a "place" inside each of us that "knows" the truth. Philosophers, scientists and even religious people agree that experiences beyond reason, such as those involving near death, impact people the greatest. It is during those moments "The Truth" is revealed.

The "place" of the whole truth is accessible by the Spirit of Truth. Partial truths and mediocrity is the condition of the unconverted mind and it is responsible for religion.

The Holy Spirit is speaking to you even now to ask Him for the living water. He will gladly give you a drink because He knows you will become heavens worshipper on earth.

Is the picture clear? The Kingdom of heaven is raining and reigning on earth. It is the living water that activates your spirit for a real encounter with Christ. It is His Spirit who will lead you into "all truth" and stimulate your thirst.

Beholding Jesus is only possible after the Spirit gives you living water. The word beholding is not mere looking but it implies comprehension, which means to have revelatory knowledge and understanding of the object.

Picture a person dying of thirst in a desert. If the body is introduced to the liquid elements of H_2O the organs are reborn and what was dying just a short while ago, is energized with life. Jesus is the water, both physically and spiritually for life.

Those who have not entered The Kingdom will neither see Him nor understand His words. I am talking about a real transformation not a perceived or psychological experience, which yields little tangible change. Most church people, listening to the words of man, remain sick, poor and frightened because there spirits are dry and dying.

Most people's spirits are dying and lifeless. Our spirit knows the truth, but it has no strength or power to lead a rebellion against the structures of the mind and soul.

After the living water enters, something miraculous happens. Heaven invades the spirit with light and the life of man.

In Him was Life, and that Life was the Light of men.

John 1:4 KJV

The Father, the One who said, "Light Is," illuminates your spirit to the truth. Immediately your spiritual eyes and ears are open and the prophetic is activated.

For God, who said Let light shine out of darkness, is the one who shined in our hearts to give us the light of the glorious knowledge of God in the face of Christ.

2 Corinthians 4:6 NET

A successful journey from a child to a mature son requires the Holy Spirit. Thank God for Jesus. His life and words while on the earth are the timeless treasures to sonship hidden for each generation to search out as the pearl of great price.

My life has changed dramatically by practicing what I have shared in these writings. The day the Holy Spirit began to show me Christ as the living water, both physically and spiritually, heaven opened and I heard the voice of God say, *"receive Nathaniel's anointing."*

Philip came across Nathanael and said to him, We have made a discovery! It is he of whom Moses, in the law, and the prophets were writing, Jesus of Nazareth, the son of Joseph.

Nazareth! said Nathanael, Is it possible for any good to come out of Nazareth? Philip said to him, Come and see.

Jesus saw Nathanael coming to him and said of him, See, here is a true son of Israel in whom there is nothing false.

Nathanael said to him, Where did you get knowledge of me? In answer Jesus said, Before Philip was talking with you, while you were still under the fig-tree, I saw you.

Nathanael said to him, Rabbi, you are the Son of God, you are King of Israel!

In answer Jesus said to him, You have faith because I said to you, I saw you under the fig-tree. You will see greater things than these.

And he said to him, Truly I say to you all, You will see heaven opening and God's angels going up and coming down on the Son of man.

John 1:45-51 BBE

Jesus chose His disciples, but they needed to choose Him as well. This is the condition of mankind. God chose to reconcile the world with Himself, but He will not force anyone to accept it.

Nathaniel is drawn to Jesus because of the prophetic. The prophetic character of Jesus manifested through His words and thoughts. He was "in the Father" and the Father was "in Him." He was prophetically connected at all times with heaven. When we are conscious of Christ, His prophetic character will be manifested in our thoughts, actions and society.

The character of Nathaniel qualified Him to see the unseen. The Holy Spirit opens heaven to anyone with no guile. The word guile means innocent or a heart with no deceit.

Love is attracted and emits a frequency protecting those with God's glory. Furthermore, it allows those with that vibration to see and hear the wonders of heaven.

Our character should attract love and an open heaven. We must be harmless as doves and wise as serpents in the earth. The Lord spoke to me many years ago and told me to be less conscious of myself and more conscious of His Spirit and my life would change. I believe that instruction is for all of mankind if they want to know the one who loves them more than they can possibly love themselves.

D. TRUE DISCIPLESHIP

Jesus specifically defines the word disciple as it relates to those whose desire is to imitate Him. Over the centuries the definition has remained, but the purposes have changed. Most churches have been more interested in perpetuating their doctrines and forms, than relying on the Holy Spirit.

Discipleship is the gateway to the spiritual realm and is the only physical action required by those willing to enter. There are many religions which require its disciples to separate from the world and live austerely. Unfortunately, in most cases, this is form without substance since the holy books they study and follow are not the living word.

This is not to say the Holy Spirit will not visit those whose desire is to meet Jesus. He is not religious and will meet all who call upon Him. His model for discipleship is simple; separate yourself from the false securities of the visible world so He can open your spiritual eyes.

One of the goals of this book is to equip you with a revelation of Christ that will provoke a perpetual earthquake in every area of your life. Piercing the illusions in your life enabling you to see and hear instructions from the Spirit of God.

Those preoccupied with "their reality" or satisfied with their lives will not be interested in making the steps to transition into Christ. Indeed, to them the Bible will not make any sense nor be taken serious.

The Bible is a codebook written to those who have been inducted into the authors' mentality and resources. The Kingdom of heaven is Christ. His authority is released supernaturally in those hidden in Him.

The churches are filled with people who must rely on others to translate or interpret the scriptures. That is the hallmark of religion and will not produce the mind of Christ. As was said earlier, only disciples are allowed to experience the mysteries of The Kingdom.

Then the disciples came to Him and said, Why do You speak to them in parables?

96

And He replied to them, to you it has been given to know the secrets and mysteries of the kingdom of heaven, but to them it has not been given.

For whoever has [spiritual knowledge], to him will more be given and he will be furnished richly so that he will have abundance; but from him who has not, even what he has will be taken away.

This is the reason that I speak to them in parables: because having the power of seeing, they do not see; and having the power of hearing, they do not hear, nor do they grasp and understand.

In them indeed is the process of fulfillment of the prophecy of Isaiah, which says: You shall indeed hear and hear but never grasp and understand; and you shall indeed look and look but never see and perceive.

For this nation's heart has grown gross (fat and dull), and their ears heavy and difficult of hearing, and their eyes they have tightly closed, lest they see and perceive with their eyes, and hear and comprehend the sense with their ears, and grasp and understand with their heart, and turn and I should heal them.

Matthew 13:10-15 AMP

Jesus said in essence, only my disciples are given the understanding to the secrets of My Kingdom. Consider that statement.

Jesus is speaking about wisdom beyond practical understanding or philosophical interpretation. He is talking about a Kingdom not visible or attainable by the senses. Our senses are not adequate to see and hear The Kingdom. Furthermore, the mind is dull, although it was constructed to understand a different dimension.

Look at the phrase from Isaiah, which says, "turn and heal." One of the definitions of heal is to restore purity or integrity. God is waiting for us to change our ideas, thoughts and images of reality so He can restore us to purity and integrity.

Jesus, through His sacrifice, healed us completely in our spirit, soul and body. That is the salvation for all men. However, unless we are converted through repentance (changing our idea of righteousness) our spiritual eyes will remain blind to the finished work.

We have already discussed the spiritual transition into Christ via the water and Spirit. That transition is called being *born again* or entering The Kingdom of heaven. I believe Jesus restores us from our pasts or heals those who enter The Kingdom.

Religion forces people to conform to an organization rather than to depend on the Spirit. The method becomes the structures, which shape their consciousness. In other words, if someone speaks about a dog we picture our dog as the point of reference. Notice the following scripture spoken by Jesus:

> *Jesus therefore was saying to those Jews who had believed Him, If you abide in My word, then you are*

truly disciples of Mine; and you shall know the truth, and the truth shall make you free.

John 8:31-32 NASB

I have heard many preachers use these verses out of context. Jesus is the Word, which means abiding IN HIM. If anyone desires to know the truth they must first know the Word, not just scripture.

The devil uses our past memories and beliefs to stop our minds and thoughts from being converted. Until we are free from the past as our "reality" of Christ, Church, truth, freedom or being *born again*, we will not change.

Our minds are created to access and operate within the spiritual dimension and it requires more than five senses. **I believe Christ consciousness is "knowing" without learning.**

In other words, those whose minds have entered Christ are no longer subject to the laws and regulations of traditional education. The realm of the supernatural is the norm, not the exception.

And be made new in the spirit of your mind.

Ephesians 4:23

Being "in Christ" is outside of time and traditional learning. Faith is required to enter that dimension which is the only reality in the vast universe. Men are unable to measure or calculate its whereabouts, but it remains the pure substance of Christ for those same reasons.

Now faith is the substance of things hoped for, the evidence of things not seen.

Hebrews 11:1 KJV

It is precisely that substance, faith, which enables our minds to grasp the power and authority Jesus offers to those who become a disciple. We become joint heirs with the King. Do you understand why the criteria must be so stringent?

The definition of a disciple is defined by Jesus and in essence says, (paraphrasing) "we must be unaffected by the illusions of this world." Those who form attachments with the visible world are the ones most easily deceived.

Whoever comes to me and does not hate father and mother, wife and children, brothers and sisters, yes, and even life itself, cannot be my disciple.

Whoever does not carry the cross and follow me cannot be my disciple.

So therefore, none of you can become my disciple if you do not give up all your possessions.

Luke 14:26-27:33 KJV

This is serious business. No one can be transformed or receive kingship if they have attachments to the physical world. Nothing from the physical dimension can influence those who truly want to be converted.

The truth requires dying to all our perceptions of reality. We loose the right to form or express opinions. **We must either trust Him or blame someone else for our failures the rest of our lives.**

Only disciples have the ability to hear and see the spirit realm. Why? Jesus paid the horrible price in order for the Father to send His Spirit so you and I can live in Him and He in us. If we live in The Truth we see the truth and have fellowship with the Father.

That is the pearl of great price. Solomon said not to cast your pearls to the swine, as they would not value them. Disciples treasure the pearl and have paid their price.

E. DISCIPLESHIP BEGINS AT THE CROSS

Disciples have converted their minds from Adam to enter Christ. The journey into the mind of Christ begins at the cross. The cross is the symbol and reminder of submission. He paid a price we would never pay.

The cross is more than a symbol of pain and suffering. It is my reproach each time I am asked to sacrifice my time or money. It is my reminder each time I choose the illusion of sickness and disease over the stripes He took for my divine health. The cross is my admonition of His strength through submission. The cross is my power over fear in the darkest hours. The cross is the light in a world that loves darkness and prefers lies. The cross is my minds resource to break every illusion the devil presents.

We must run to the cross and remove the images we have formed as a result of religion. Once there, nail the desires and images of pain and suffering to it until the reality of life "in Christ" surges through your cells and mind. Faith will replace the spirit of fear and faith will flood your soul. **Death is no longer your worst fear, but becomes your greatest tool for facing the devil's strongest threats and illusions**.

Disciples willingly become a public display for every power and principality to see the transfer of allegiance from Adam to Christ.

This power is available to anyone who willingly allows the Spirit to nail him or her to the cross. You will have no power if you separate yourself from the One there. Jesus was not crucified to generate pity or empathy.

Religion views the crucifixion from the eyes of a spectator. The results may be emotional and lead to a greater desire to understand the love that led to such a horrible death.

But if you do not assume your responsibility in that death your mind will never change. A disciple is one who recognizes their role in driving the nails in His hands and feet. The mind of Adam is not divine, but vain, and attempts to justify its condition as the murderer of The Christ.

Religion is standing at the foot of the cross today making an effort to understand the supernatural with the mind of Adam. A mind that has been deceived and confused since the beginning of time will never be an overcomer.

The more **we try** to extricate ourselves from the trap, which is our thoughts, the tighter the noose becomes around our necks. Men run to one expert after the other, only to find the same lies dressed in a different outfit.

Jesus says in John 12:32 *"if I be lifted up from the earth I am then able to draw all men to me."* Notice, He said, *"from the earth."* Men have viewed Jesus hanging on the cross from the earth assuming their minds to be on the same plane as His.

If our view remains as a spectator on the earth the same spirit that controlled Adam will control us. Therefore, even the "nothing" or small amount of understanding about God will be removed.

> *For whoever has [spiritual knowledge], to him will more be given and he will be furnished richly so that he will have abundance; but from him who has not, even what he has will be taken away.*
> *Matthew 13:10 AMP*

Many have said abundance and wealth are trademarks of spiritual knowledge. Most churches today teach prosperity and abundance as proof of ones faith in God. Unfortunately, many more people profess to have faith in God than are wealthy. What is the problem?

Each person must determine if the knowledge he or she believes is spiritual or perceptions from the physical plane. Only the disciples have access to the spiritual wisdom of The Kingdom.

I learned something extraordinary about Jesus. The family you give away is the act, which triggers the Holy Spirit to change, not only your life, but also those you surrender. In other words, you never loose what you give Him.

A disciple follows Jesus into the waters of baptism, not as a ritual or symbol, but to complete The Kingdom transition.

CHAPTER 4

THE REFORMATION OF BAPTISM

The baptism we have traditionally understood requires the same reformation as the *born again* experience. God is concerned about form without substance, which is why He formed the earth from the living water or Christ and desires His Church to follow the same model. **The Genesis blueprint will reconnect man to his original spiritual DNA.**

God uses order to establish principles, which produce heavenly results. **The experience of *born again* followed with baptism is form with substance and produces spiritual authority.** Christ's preeminence and mysteries are intended for His disciples to share. We have discussed the price to become His disciple, but now we will experience baptism as the fruit.

The consciousness of Christ was formed in the early Church largely because of baptism. The Church has lost its voice in the earth because of following the traditions of men instead of the principles of heaven.

During the first three centuries, Roman citizens who were baptized became outcasts by loosing their property and citizenship. Nevertheless, they would line up along the riverbanks to pledge their lives to Christ in baptism, aware of the persecution that would ensue.

Persecution to the point of death is unfamiliar to most Christians in the West, but was undeniably the most important dynamic for spreading Christianity throughout the world. Furthermore, except for baptism the Bible does not speak about a public altar call to follow Jesus.

Baptism altered the consciousness of the disciple to witness the spiritual realm known as the Kingdom of Heaven. The fear of death was eliminated and indeed another level of faith flooded their souls.

The devil knew the strategy to destroy the spread of Christianity was to change the spiritual principles of God into formulas and rituals. The result is religion or form without substance and has grieved the Lord as much as Adam's betrayal.

Moses asked God thousands of years before to show him the ways of His Spirit. Moses wanted to "know" God in the way a husband and wife unite as one flesh. He knew intimacy would please God and establish order.

> *If you really are pleased with me, show me your ways so that I can **know you** and so that you will continue to be pleased with me.*

> *Exodus 33:13 GW*

If we want to know God we must do things His way and baptism is no exception. We said previously, in order to be "in Christ" we must have intimate knowledge of Him. The knowledge of God is revealed to those who follow His precepts out of love, not as a religious prescription.

A. JOHN THE BAPTIST

It was a mystery to me why John the Baptist, a priest from the lineage of Levi, would introduce baptism to the Jews. Furthermore, he made the path straight for Jesus, whom he would later baptize.

John was the last of the old covenant prophets and the greatest according to Jesus. Moreover, John was the only prophet, aside from Jesus, whose birth was prophesied in the scriptures. (*Malachi 3:1 Isaiah 40:3*)

> *But why did you go out? to see a prophet? Yes, I say to you, and more than a prophet.*
>
> *This is he of whom it has been said, See, I send my servant before your face, who will make ready your way before you.*
>
> *Truly I say to you, among the sons of women there has not been a greater than John the Baptist: but he who is least in the kingdom of heaven is greater than he.*
>
> *Matthew 11:9-11 BBE*

John knew the Law and the consecration requirements of washing with water prior to entering the tabernacle or dressing in the holy garments. He also knew the Levites were separated from the Jewish multitude and sanctified for service in the tabernacle by the same custom.

Our previous discussion of water and its relationship to Christ adds a new dimension to cleansing and sanctification in the scriptures. Your revelation of Christ will be enhanced each time you see Him as the physical and spiritual waters of the word.

> *You shall bring Aaron and his sons to the door of the Tent of Meeting and wash them with water.*
>
> *You shall put on Aaron the holy garments, and anoint and consecrate him, so he may serve Me as priest.*
>
> *Exodus 40:12-13 AMP*

> *Take the Levites out from among the children of Israel and make them clean.*
> *And this is how you are to make them clean: let the holy water which takes away sin be put on them, and let the hair all over their bodies be cut off with a sharp blade, and let their clothing be washed and their bodies made clean.*
>
> *Numbers 8:6-7 BBE*

Baptism was God's demand for a higher level of consecration than the Old Testament laws concerning the washing of the priests.

The Jews believed circumcision was their mark of blessing, but had forgotten their responsibility of sanctification. God gave the following instructions before the promises and blessings.

When Abram was ninety-nine years old, the Lord appeared to him and said, I am the Almighty God; walk and live habitually before Me and be perfect (blameless, wholehearted, complete).

Genesis 17:1 AMP

Circumcision was to remind the Jews they were chosen to represent God's sinless nature in the earth. The Messiah was the fruit of God's covenant but their hearts and stiff necks would make them reject and murder their own deliverer.

This is My covenant, which you shall keep, between Me and you and your posterity after you: Every male among you shall be circumcised.

And you shall circumcise the flesh of your foreskin, and it shall be a token or sign of the covenant (the promise or pledge) between Me and you.

He who is eight days old among you shall be circumcised, every male throughout your generations,

Genesis 17:10-12 AMP

The Law required male children to be circumcised on the eighth day. Infant baptism was subsequently ordained in Churches around the world as a result of this practice. There is no rationale for that practice and it is one of the strategies the devil has used to undermine and destroy the true power in baptism.

God hates religion and He instructed John to warn the Pharisees and Sadducees who came to be baptized to produce fruits verifying their hearts circumcision or run from God's judgment.

Circumcise yourselves to the Lord and take away the foreskins of your hearts, you men of Judah and inhabitants of Jerusalem, lest My wrath go forth like fire [consuming all that gets in its way] and burn so that no one can quench it because of the evil of your doings.

Jeremiah 4:4 AMP

But when he saw many of the Pharisees and Sadducees coming for baptism, he said to them, You brood of vipers! Who warned you to flee and escape from the wrath and indignation [of God against disobedience] that is coming?

Bring forth fruit that is consistent with repentance [let your lives prove your change of heart];

Matthew 3:7-8 AMP

John was bridging the old and new covenants with the waters of Christ. He was proclaiming the message of The Kingdom with a greater revelation of power and universal authority. John was not a high priest, but he was about to baptize our High Priest and in so doing, ministered to the Holy of Holies.

Therefore, John announced a better revelation and consecration than the previous generation because he was filled with the Holy Ghost, while in his mothers' womb.

And when the voice of Mary came to the ears of Elisabeth, the baby made a sudden move inside her; then Elisabeth was full of the Holy Spirit.

Luke 1:42 BBE

One of the most important indications of being filled with the Spirit is prophesying. The language of the Spirit transforms both the physical and spiritual worlds.

The mark of a prophet is determined by the revelation of Christ he reveals. In order for the progressive revelation of Jesus to increase, each generation must repent from their current level of righteousness and change to the new one being revealed.

Jesus brought The Kingdom in His physical body because of prophecy. John was sent to baptize those who would hear the prophetic voice and change.

I baptize you with water so that you will change the way you think and act. But the one who comes after me is more powerful than I. I am not worthy to remove his sandals. He will baptize you with the Holy Spirit and fire.

Matthew 3:11 GWORD

It is no different today than it was in John's time. Religion has made a form and ritual out of the supernatural words of Christ, including baptism.

Religious people are satisfied with their revelation of God and are precisely the ones Prophets must endure to fulfill their call. The persecution from those who refuse repentance is the fire used to baptize us and destroy them.

111

B. JOHN BAPTIZES JESUS

Why did John baptize Jesus? According to the Law the candidate had to be thirty years of age before entering the priesthood. John was a Levite the son of a priest, who was struck mute by an angel because of unbelief.

John was both a priest and anointed by the Holy Spirit at birth authorizing his earthly and spiritual position according to heaven and Jewish Law.

John immersed Jesus as a visible sign of separation from the congregation of Israel into the priesthood according to the Law of Moses.

> *Then Jesus came from Galilee to John at the Jordan, to be given baptism by him. But John would have kept him back, saying, It is I who have need of baptism from you, and do you come to me?*
>
> *But Jesus made answer, saying to him, Let it be so now: because so it is right for us to make righteousness complete.*
>
> *Matthew 3:13-15 BBE*

John knew who Jesus was, but did not understand the spiritual significance behind the act. Many in churches today know Jesus to be the Son of God, but do not know the power of baptism. John was not a high priest by lineage and as such, was not allowed to minister in the Holy of Holies. Nevertheless, because he was ordaining Christ, who is our Holy of Holies, God promoted him to high priest.

For every high priest is taken from among the people and appointed to represent them before God, to offer both gifts and sacrifices for sins.

Hebrews 5:1 NET

Moreover, Jesus was of the bloodline of David making him not only a high priest, but also a king. Jesus by virtue of John's baptism and His lineage, became a Royal High Priest after the order of Melchizedek.

So also Christ did not glorify himself in becoming high priest, but the one who glorified him was God, who said to him, You are my Son! Today I have fathered you, as also in another place God says, You are a priest forever in the order of Melchizedek.

Hebrews 5:5-6 NET

Being named by God a high priest of the order of Melchizedek.
Hebrews 5:10 BBE

Jesus knew the earthly and heavenly significance of the baptism by John. Jesus became the Jews High Priest with all the power bestowed upon Aaron and Moses. He was the spiritual High Priest after Melchizedek, which authorizes Him to baptize us into His Spirit, thereby, fulfilling "all righteousness."

C. JESUS BAPTIZED INTO CHRIST

The spiritual significance of that event is even more astounding than words and is our inheritance once we are *born again*.

We must understand Jesus was not born "the Christ" or the source for our salvation. He was born into a physical body with a soul contaminated from the first Adam. His spirit was and is God, but it (His spirit) had to dominate the body and soul, the same as all men. *But for / purpose esste ahuly was therefor our Salvation*

Although he was a son, he learned obedience through the things he suffered.
And by being perfected in this way, he became the source of eternal salvation to all who obey him,

Hebrews 5:8-9 NET

The power of salvation is different from the authority of being born into Christ. Jesus purchased salvation for all men and it is available to whoever will call upon Him. The thief dying next to Jesus on the cross received salvation because he believed Him to be the Son. He was not *born again* because he was not immersed into Christ. The description Jesus explained to Nicodemus is, "immersed into Him" and is available to disciples today.

After He came up from the water in the Jordan, the Holy Spirit rested, overshadowed or hovered on Him and the Father spoke.

After being baptized, Jesus came up immediately from the water; and behold, the heavens were opened, and he saw the Spirit of God descending as a dove and lighting on Him,

and behold, a voice out of the heavens said, This is My beloved Son, in whom I am well-pleased.

Matthew 3:16-17 NAS

The model used at creation was forming the second Adam, but this time there would be no chance for failure. **Jesus understood the element of water was more than liquid, it was His soul's consciousness of Christ. Jesus was immersed into His Spirit. At that instant he became one with the Father and the Spirit in the element of Himself.**

He was in the beginning with God. All things came into being through Him, and apart from Him nothing that exists came into being.
John 1:2-3 WEY

It was at that instant heaven opened and the second Adam emerged with all the power of heaven. **His spirit was one with the Holy Spirit and He and the Father's word became one as it was before the foundation of the world.** More importantly for us, He became the eternal spring of living water.

The heavenly blueprint to reproduce God Sons in the earth was established and sealed with the baptism of Jesus. The living water is the spiritual womb into The Kingdom of God. God's word is His incorruptible seed and the Holy Spirit is the person who impregnates our spirits. Baptism is designed to release heaven into our spirit, soul and body the same way it did Jesus.

The transition had taken place between the old and new covenants. Jesus was both sinless man and God. His Kingdom transcended the visible and invisible dimensions simultaneously by the Holy Spirit. A temple not made with hands in order for each generation to grow in the revelation of Christ and His Kingdom authority.

His baptism was the signed contract with heaven of His commitment to go to the cross to "fulfill all righteousness" and finish what had been decided before the foundation of the world.

It is true that He was chosen and foreordained (destined and foreknown for it) before the foundation of the world, but He was brought out to public view (made manifest) in these last days (at the end of the times) for the sake of you.

Peter 1:20 AMP

Baptism must be conducted the way heaven ordained it, in order for the same power to be released. The model has been corrupted through out history. God is releasing a new reformation and sending prophets to make the crooked straight.

D. SINGLE IMMERSION

John baptized in the name of Jehovah or God the Father. This was because he was preparing the way for the one who had not yet arrived.

John's baptism was a single immersion into the Fathers forgiveness of those who confessed their unrighteousness and willingness to be transformed. This baptism was for those whose minds had been converted from the dead works of religious sacrifices and the hypocrisy associated with circumcision. John was the forerunner of The Kingdom and was reconciling a remnant whose hearts and minds were committed to the coming Christ.

John's time on earth was coming to a close because he had fulfilled his purpose and calling.

They came to John and said to him, Rabbi, the one who was with you across the Jordan, to whom you testified, here he is baptizing, and all are going to him.

John answered, No one can receive anything except what has been given from heaven.

You yourselves are my witnesses that I said, I am not the Messiah, but I have been sent ahead of him.

He who has the bride is the bridegroom. The friend of the bridegroom, who stands and hears him, rejoices greatly at the bridegroom's voice.

For this reason my joy has been fulfilled.

He must increase, but I must decrease.

John 3:30 NASV

John's pure heart and clear purpose are reflected in the scripture above. If you want to live a life filled with joy allow Him to increase, while you decrease. John had proved himself a worthy Son of God and was recognized by Jesus for his work.

The transition between John and Jesus was physical, as well as spiritual, and demonstrates the ways of God. John was the prophetic head of God's remnant Church on the earth prior to Jesus' baptism. The transition required a change in headship, as well as covenants.

Immediately she hurried back to the king and made her request: I want the head of John the Baptist on a platter immediately.

Mark 6:25 WEY

And he is the head of the body, the church: who is the beginning, the firstborn from the dead; that in all things he might have the preeminence.

Colossians 1:18 ASV

The eternal Son was now the head over the Church forever and His Kingdom would never end. The head of Christ would never be deceived or rebel against the Father. The mind of Christ is the consciousness of God whose image and likeness would be on those who were *born again* and baptized into Christ.

E. SUBMERGED TWICE

Baptism in the early church was different in form and as a result, produced a much different Christian than today. My understanding and revelation of Christ as both physical and spiritual water led me to research the history of baptism. The results will shock you as it has me. Most importantly, these revelations will change your understanding and commitment to Christ profoundly.

The characteristic of the Godhead is the distinction between the baptism of John and Jesus not just transition between the old and new covenant. John's baptism was into the Father, while Jesus baptized His disciples into the Father and His own name.

Jesus required repentance and faith in God the Father and Himself. He was the co-creator of all things and Messiah to the Jews. Those who accepted Jesus, as Christ, would be immersed twice. The baptisms were into the Father, as John preached and the Son of God.

Paul describes the difference between the two baptisms in Acts 19:

> *And he said, Into what then were you baptized? And they said, Into John's baptism.*

> *Paul said, John baptized with the baptism of repentance, telling the people to believe in Him who was coming after him, that is, in Jesus.*

> *When they heard this, they were baptized in the name of the Lord Jesus.*

> *Acts 19:3-5 NAS*

I would like to quote *John G. Lake,* one of the most renowned healers of modern times concerning the practice of dual immersions.

"I have spent twenty years going into the matter and with perhaps one exception, so far as I know, I have probably spent more time on this issue than anyone alive. I met with Reverend Edward Kennedy, whose writings on the subject of baptism are regarded as the best in modern time. He referred me to the writings of the early Fathers. I found their writings at the British Museum in London, which supported my belief of the dual baptism of Jesus while on earth. Furthermore, it went on to say, the early Fathers had distinctly recognized the difference between the baptism of John and Jesus and declared the baptism of Jesus was dual into the name of the Son; the candidate being immersed in water twice not once."[1]

In my opinion the subject of dual baptism is relative because it demonstrates an ever-increasing influence of the Godhead on earth and in men. The power to overcome the enemy is not in form, but substance. Jesus knew the significance of following God's form because of love. Love is the substance in the form, which defeats evil first inside us and then our surroundings.

Dual baptisms were only practiced while He was on the earth. After His resurrection He instructed the disciples to baptize into the complete Godhead. This was the only time He gave instructions on the proper way to seal one's immersion into The Kingdom.

---

[1] *John G. Lake, The Complete Collection of His Life Teachings by Roberts Liardon, Albury Publishing, ISBN 1-57778-075-2, page 187*

F. IMMERSED INTO THE FULL GODHEAD

In order to reestablish the ways of God, it will be helpful to demonstrate the pattern and practice of the early Church. I want to repeat, I am not interested in methodology or formulas. My purpose is to bring back the principals of Christ, in order to change men into God's champions in the earth.

The following articles will confirm the practice of the early church was to immerse the candidates into the names of the Godhead, three separate times. This was the method until Pope Gregory in 633 A.D., changed the practice to single immersion.

Here is a quote from Saint Basil the Great (330-379) "— one of the most important saints of the Orthodox church: This great sign of baptism is fulfilled in three immersions, with three invocations, so that the image of death might be completely formed, and the newly-baptized might have their souls enlightened with divine knowledge. "[2]

Here is a quote from the Apostolical Constitutions written 200 A.D.:

"If any bishop or presbyter does not perform the three immersions of the one admission, but one immersion, which is given into the death of Christ, let him be deprived; for the Lord did not say, "Baptize into my death," but, "Go ye and make disciples of all nations, baptizing them into the name of the Father, and of the Son, and of the Holy Ghost."

Do ye, therefore, O bishops, baptize thrice into one Father, and Son, and Holy Ghost, according to the will of Christ, and our constitution by the Spirit?"[3]

---

[2] *St. Basil the Great, On The Holy Spirit, page 59*

[3] *Apostolical Constitutions, Ante-Nicene Christian Library, vol. 17, p. 263*

"Baptize into the name of the Father and of the Son and of the Holy Spirit in living (running) water. But if they have not living water, baptize into other water; and if thou canst not in cold, in warm" (baptisate eis to onoma tou patos kai tou huiou kai tou hagiou pneumatos en hudati zonti). "But if thou have not either, pour out water thrice (tris) upon the head into the name of the Father and Son and Holy Spirit."[4]

Here the triple action is maintained throughout, even in clinical baptism, while immersion is the rule.

"And indeed it is not only once but three times that we are immersed into the Three Persons, at each several mention of their names" (nam nec semel, sed ter, ad singula nomina, in personas singulos, tinguimur)."[5]

Introduced single immersion "into the death of Christ." This innovation was condemned. Apostolical Constitutions, 50, says, "If any presbyter or bishop does not perform the one initiation with three immersions, but with giving one immersion only into the death of the Lord, let him be deposed."[6]

Single immersion was allowed by Gregory the Great (circa 691) to the church in Spain in opposition to the Arians who used a trine (not triune) immersion. This was exceptional.

The greek church has always baptized by triune immersion. The historical practice of the Christian church may well be summed up in the words of Dean Stanley: "There can be no question that the original form of baptism — the very meaning

---

[4] *The Didache (100-150 A.D.) Chapter VII*

[5] *Tertullian*

[6] *Eunomius (circa 360) Epis., i.43*

of the word — was complete immersion in the deep baptismal waters; and that for at least four centuries, any other form was either unknown, or regarded, unless in the case of dangerous illness, as an exceptional, almost monstrous case ... A few drops of water are now the western substitute for the threefold plunge into the rushing river or the wide baptisteries of the East."[7]

For the first three centuries the most universal practice of baptism was "... that those who were baptized, were plunged, submerged, immersed into the water"[8]

Jesus is very precise when choosing His words. He introduces the third person of the God Head as the complete and full measure of heavenly baptism.

There can be no doubt of the significance and importance of these instructions from our Lord. Neither can there be any resistance to being immersed three separate times.

Jesus however came near and said to them, All power in Heaven and over the earth has been given to me.

---

[7] *Greek Church History of Eastern Church, 28*

[8] *Christian Institutions, p. 21James Quinter, Triune Immersion as the Apostolic Form of Christian Baptism; C. F. Yoder, God's Means of Grace, Brethren Pub. House, Elgin, Ill., U.S.A.; Smith, Dict. of Christian Antiquities; Hastings, ERE; Bible Dicts.; Church Fathers; Church Histories, and Histories of Baptism. (All of these documents are copied from the public domain of crosswire)*

Go therefore and make disciples of all the nations; baptize (baptizo[9]) them into the name of the Father, and of the Son, and of the Holy Spirit,

and teach them to obey every command which I have given you. And remember, I am with you always, day by day, until the Close of the Age.

Matthew 28:18-20 WEY

Jesus is commanding an allegiance and undying faith in God the Father, God the Son and God the Holy Spirit illustrated by immersion into each of their characters and natures.

Kingdom baptism is both physical and spiritual immersion into the nature and character of the Father, Son and Holy Ghost. The revelation we have discovered about the "living water" changes the dynamics about water being only physical.

I believe, as well as practice submerging those who bear fruits of conversion into The Kingdom of God. Immersing each disciple into the God Head has proven to be a very powerful tool for changing a ritual into the revelation of Christ.

Furthermore, I am convinced the authority and power released spiritually through immersion into the Father, Son and Holy Spirit obliterates the sin consciousness once and for all.

In the following scripture, I believe Peter is speaking about The Kingdom baptism into the character of the Holy Spirit.

---

[9] *The Greek word used by Jesus for baptism is baptizo, which means repeatedly immersed.*

Who, in the days of Noah, went against God's orders; but God in his mercy kept back the punishment, while Noah got ready the ark, in which a small number, that is to say eight persons, got salvation through water:

And baptism, of which this is an image, now gives you salvation, not by washing clean the flesh, but by making you free from the sense of sin before God, through the coming again of Jesus Christ from the dead;

Who has gone into heaven, and is at the right hand of God, angels and authorities and powers having been put under his rule.

1 Peter 3:20-22 BBE

Peter describes a baptism of power to go through the storm not to escape it. The consciousness of man is changed by the triune baptism into the Godhead. The power the Church is missing resides in following the principals Christ instituted in baptism. Peter is describing salvation as the water of Christ. The power over sin is in the Godhead. The triune immersion is the act, which changes our consciousness from sin to salvation.

The final authority over powers and principalities is after Jesus baptizes us with the Holy Spirit. The immersion into the Godhead empowers us over sin consciousness. The fire of the Holy Spirit is an ever-increasing baptism, which is administered by Christ.

But you shall receive power (ability, efficiency, and

might) when the Holy Spirit has come upon you, and you shall be My witnesses in Jerusalem and all Judea and Samaria and to the ends (the very bounds) of the earth.

Acts 1:8 AMP

Baptized in the Spirit is an invisible submersion with visible results beyond "speaking in tongues." The mark of this baptism resides in the spiritual dimensions. Those truly baptized with the Holy Spirit are not satisfied with their present knowledge of Christ. They are marked with a hunger and passion to change the status quo. They are not people of reputation or recognition, but many times are the ones interceding for the next generations.

Many of them are before the Lord night and day praying for mercy and grace over their countries and nations. Their lives are dedicated in the pursuit of knowing Christ and His Spirit in deeper and more profound ways. They are the ones praying for us right now.

Baptism is not a ritual and if understood correctly can change society. The words of Christ are carefully chosen concerning the principals of being *born again* and baptism. God will wait for a generation that will change ceremonies and formulas into their intended purposes.

I would like to describe my experiences as it relates to baptism. It is not meant to be a pattern or blueprint.

It is my story and although for me dramatic and profound each persons will be different. One can never know the reality of Christ through books and teachings. He is forever changing and

126

each marvelous characteristic is more exciting and exhilarating than the last.

The journey into Christ is eternal. Those who are willing to renounce everything and trust the following words of Jesus are eligible to taste the goodness of God.

Jesus said to him, I am the way, and the truth, and the life: no man comes to the Father, but by Me.

John 14:6 KJV

G. MY BAPTISM EXPERIENCE

When The Spirit revealed Jesus to me as the spiritual and physical "water" I was visiting the Jordan River. I immediately made the decision to practice what I had just learned.

My body and spirit "vibrated" at the mere thought of consciously stepping into the same body of water Jesus chose to consummate His commitment to the Father. At that instant, I was touching more than water. I was stepping into Jesus Himself. His body, thoughts, emotions, tears and joys were encompassing my feet in what I identified as water, but it was actually burning my feet.

My heart raced, while my mind showed me an image of water circling a drain in a sink. It was as if everything inside of me was being delivered from theology and preconceived ideas. I could see my "religious life" emptying down the basin of my mind.

At some point, heaven opened and I had a vision of Jesus

entering the Jordan. As I watched, it appeared as if Jesus was entering the liquid substance of water, but as He walked the water began to shine until it was brighter than the sun. It appeared as if Jesus was being immersed in Christ.

Jesus was and is The Christ. However, He was born into the body and souls condition of the first Adam. His physical birth and sinless life is what gives Him all authority and power.

Jesus had to become The Christ in His soul and body. As Jesus walked into the water of the Jordan, He united heaven and earth with "The knowledge" of Christ consciousness, thus transforming H_2O into the heavenly substance. What knowledge you ask?

The knowledge of creation, which said, "In the beginning God created." Jesus stepped into the substance that represented timeless, formless eternity. He Is, Was and Will be. Water is the conduit to the eternal beginning that He alone had access because of His submission to His Father's purpose.

The Lord reveals hidden treasures to all those who would be converted into His Kingdom. Access to the riches of The Kingdom is hidden inside our willingness to submit to His purpose.

Those in lack or diseased in mind or body are not fulfilling their destinies. You must make the decision to enter Christ.

If you are in Christ you have lost your right for an opinion or decision. The Holy Spirit will lead you into the wilderness, in order for you to complete your submission. Once you pass that test, He will guide you into victory 100% of the time. The test will last as long as you insist in having your own way.

128

Many who believe they are Christians are living a false perception of reality. Their lives will not change regardless of the church they belong to or the people who pray for them.

During my baptism my name was submerged into His. He gave me a name that He uses on special occasions. I became His beloved for eternity. I had no concern for tomorrow or yesterday. My only purpose was to please Him! The life I knew lost all meaning and purpose.

The joy I have found over the years has been in discovering how much I mean to Him. Have you had that experience? He longs to make you His forever. He alone has the power to make you safe and secure.

I believe the baptism Jesus desires is the immersion into each person of the Godhead. The Father, Son and Holy Spirit. My experience was beyond anything I had imagined or could dream. A magnificent wave of light engulfed my heart each time my body was submerged into another member of the Godhead. I experienced a rush of emotions and knowledge with each immersion into the Divine personality complete with a revelation of their characters and nature.

I was baptized into God the Father and experienced a love for human beings like never before. I wanted to produce and reproduce sons in His image. Love was the overwhelming power that immersed my heart and soul.

As I was baptized in Jesus Name, the nature of the Son was revealed. I instantly witnessed submission and obedience from heavens perspective. Jesus revealed a character and nature of Himself I had never seen or heard. **The power of obedience**

and the strength of submission opened heaven and revealed the authority hidden from the world.

The experience of immersion in the Holy Ghost released a revelation of the power Jesus told His disciples to go to Jerusalem to wait on. My spirit was immersed in The Spirit exposing eternity to my consciousness and the understanding of the end from the beginning.

The water I was under became the life and the living Christ in every pore of my body. I was submerged in physical water but my soul and spirit were being illuminated with a substance I can only describe as a glorious light.

I was reminded that Jesus stepped into the Jordan for reasons we previously described, but something even more powerful happened. As I said earlier, I believe Jesus is the "living water" both physically and spiritually.

The sinless Jesus was immersed in the perfect Christ uniting His spirit with His soul and body. He was perfected and became the author of eternal salvation. (Hebrews 5:9)

The Christ was made the perfect Son and second Adam through his baptism. Heaven and earth were reunited in Him as in the beginning at creation.

Remember, immediately after surfacing from the water heaven opened and the Holy Spirit descended on Him and God the Father introduced His Son.

Heavens' "Word" was immersed inside earth's H_2O. The

witness spoken of in *1 John 5* was being fulfilled on many levels.

For there are three that bear record in heaven, the Father, the Word, and the Holy Ghost: and these three are one.

And there are three that bear witness in earth, the Spirit, and the water, and the blood: and these three agree in one.

1 John 5:7-8 KJV

The same Word that created the heavens and earth was immersed in the element He had created from heaven. The Kingdom of heaven was in earth as it was in heaven. The baptism on earth was truly a heavenly immersion, not a symbolic ritual.

The brief time I was underwater the Lord immersed me in a heavenly vision before the foundation of the world to show me the One who Is and Was and Is to come. The timeless dimension in Christ is NOW because the past and future have been completed in Him.

I had a glimpse of the experience Paul writes about in the following verse:

And I know that this man (whether in the body or apart from the body I do not know, God knows)
was caught up into paradise and heard things too sacred to be put into words, things that a person is not permitted to speak.

2 Corinthians 12: 3-4 NET

I am unable to convey fully the experiences of that event but the Lord did instruct me to be the living water in this dying world. He said, *I would exalt those whose character demonstrates meekness and patience. Do not be weary in well doing, but drink deep and often from My Spirit.*

Furthermore, He said, *never to be afraid or surprised by events on the planet, but to be immoveable and unshakeable in the times ahead. In addition, the end and the beginning had been written before the foundation of the world and those whose focus is on tribulation and anti-Christ would miss what He has prepared for those who love Him today.* u agree

CHAPTER 5

"THAT DAY" IS NOW

Many scientist and religious leaders speak about a time and a "day" to come when man's problems will be solved. The world is looking to the future for solutions, but totally unconscious of its own spiritual condition as the source of the problems. The Church was designed to provide solutions, but instead has offered religious traditions and "after- death" theologies.

The consciousness of Adam is the problem for the circumstances and conditions of the earth. Hence, man is unable to save himself or anyone else and in order to preserve the illusion of control must promise future solutions. New dreams must be promised to the next generations to hide the failures of the past, until chaos erupts in the form of war, famine or plagues.

God knew mankind's choices and future before the foundation of the world and provided the solution from the beginning. I said Genesis was the beginning and the end. "In Christ" is the solution for all of man's toil and labor.

Genesis and Hebrews describe the journey from the old covenant to the new.

And on the seventh day God ended His work, which He had done; and He rested on the seventh day from all His work, which He had done. And God blessed (spoke good of) the seventh day, set it apart as His own, and hallowed it, because on it God rested from all His work which He had created and done.

Genesis 2:2-3 AMP

God made six days for man to complete his tasks and if finished properly would lead him to "the day" He prepared for those who love Him. Each day provides bread, forgiveness and power over evil in order to position us for "that day." The seventh day is unlike any other day because it was the only one He would inhabit.

Religion teaches us to prepare for a day of tribulation, turmoil, death and destruction before we find rest. God made the seventh day sanctified and blessed it for Himself. The word sanctified means set apart, separated or holy.

Sanctify them in your truth. Your word is truth.

John 17:17 WEB

All who have read this far hopefully understand the "Word" and Truth as Jesus. He is also the seventh day and since man was created on the sixth mankind was easily positioned to enter God's rest with little effort. The gospel message for today is the same as it was in Genesis. Jesus is ready to receive all those who will enter Him.

We have been religiously conditioned to think the "gospel" is

134

the message of Jesus dying for our sins, resurrecting, ascending to heaven and returning. No one would dispute that as the most exciting news since man's separation from God, but if that is the only definition, what is Paul talking about in Hebrews?

> *For to us was the **gospel** preached, as well as to them (the Israelites in the wilderness): but the word, which they heard, did not profit them, not being mixed with faith in them that heard it.*

> *For we who have believed do enter into rest, as he said, As I have sworn in my wrath, if they shall enter into my rest: although the works were finished from the foundation of the world.*

> *For he spoke in a certain place of the seventh day on this wise, And God rested the seventh day from all his works.*

> *And in this place again, If they shall enter into my rest.*

Hebrews 4:2-5 WEB, Author's Emphasis

Some theologians teach the gospel reference in Hebrews refers to the Promised Land. I believe that is only part of what the writer is taking about. In my opinion, the physical land of Israel will never solve their problems.

Otherwise, the following scripture would not have been added.

> *If Joshua had given them rest, he would not have*

135

said anything about another day.

So that there is still a Sabbath-keeping for the people of God.

For the man who comes into his rest has had rest from his works, as God did from his.

Hebrews 4:8-10 BBE

I believe the Holy Spirit was attempting to change the mentality of the Church of those days the way He is today. **The physical world is not the answer to our spiritual condition.** The world is spinning in its misery because they refuse to enter the rest of God in the person of Christ.

Does "rest" from our work mean quit your job and put your feet up? Of course the answer is no. The visible world is physical and so are our bodies.

For physical training is of some value (useful for a little), but godliness (spiritual training) is useful and of value in everything and in every way, for it holds promise for the present life and also for the life, which is to come.

1 Timothy 4:8 AMP

The problems in our personal lives and the physical world are the result of not understanding our spiritual nature. The Sabbath day is not a religious or calendar day of the week. It amazes me to find so many people eager to religiously follow the same rituals and customs Jesus came to destroy.

It may indicate their hunger to reproduce the power they read about in the Bible but have not experienced in today's churches. **This is mere form without substance and was why Jesus manifested and returned His Kingdom.**

The problem unfortunately is people interpret scriptures without intimacy in "The Word". For example, there are those who believe the Bible speaks about a time when God is going to rebuild His temple to sacrifice rams and bulls. The same people celebrate "holy" days including the "Sabbath." They have many scriptures to justify their actions but at the root is the belief God does not change. The following are some of the verses they cite in their defense:

> *Jesus Christ is the same yesterday and today and forever.*
> *Hebrews 13:8 NET*

> *For I the LORD do not change; therefore you, O children of Jacob, have not perished.*
> *Malachi 3:6 NRSV*

> *Since, I, the LORD, do not go back on my promises, you, sons of Jacob, have not perished.*
> *Malachi 3:6 NET*

The verse from Hebrews is also spoken by Jesus in Revelation 1:8 as the One who Is and Was and Is to come. Jesus is the Old Covenant, He is the New and He will be anything you or I need in the future to change religion into revelation of Himself. God's covenant is Jesus. He has always been the covenant, not rules, laws or any other religious systems.

God is continually changing to those whose desire is to know Him. Eternity is not measured by time and to assume God is the same because you have not progressed is silly. The Holy Spirit was sent to show us all things.

O YOU poor and silly and thoughtless and unreflecting and senseless Galatians! Who has fascinated or bewitched or cast a spell over you, unto whom—right before your very eyes—Jesus Christ (the Messiah) was openly and graphically set forth and portrayed as crucified?
Galatians 3:1 AMP

Therefore, labor to enter His rest speaks of ripping the mental veil, which has bound and restricted your spirit from knowing Christ. Picture yourself bound in the grave clothes of Lazarus and Jesus screaming your name to COME FORTH.

The effort required to rise up and battle all of the religious thoughts you have submitted your mind and body to is the labor spoken of in Hebrews.

But seek (aim at and strive after) first of all His kingdom and His righteousness (His way of doing and being right), and then all these things taken together will be given you besides.

Matthew 6:33 AMP

Jesus explained the priority of life to His disciples and in doing so described the seventh day. Jesus is the Kingdom and He is God's righteousness. Heaven and eternity begins "that day" you enter Him and His righteousness. The end of your time is when you enter the timeless One and it is mentioned in the next verse:

Again He sets a definite day, [a new] Today, [and gives another opportunity of securing that rest] saying

*through David after so long a time in the words
already quoted, Today, if you would hear His voice and
when you hear it, do not harden your hearts.*
Hebrews 4:7 AMP

That day is today and those whose hearts are open will hear a
new sound of freedom and rebirth. Then you must labor to
break all of your mental images and conditioning for birth into
Christ. The whole world is looking for deliverance from the
torment of life. Many tell me they want to know the truth and
are tired of religion. I tell them to enter into Christ and be set
free. His word is alive and will deliver you from your works if
you enter His rest.

Before creation God designed the invisible and visible worlds
to interact through Christ. Water was the medium selected and
is the instrument God still uses to nurture and care for His
creatures. **Water is a spiritual element from heaven to
ensure our physical life and spiritual connection with God.**

God designed this marvelous universe for man to discover His
wonders and ways. Nonetheless, Adam disobeyed God by
trusting his senses, producing a perpetual sin consciousness for
all generations who would follow.

Adam is the portrait of man today. He is driven by fear,
ambition and greed because his soul was corrupted with
iniquity by believing satan. **Iniquity is not sin, but the
fountain of evil that corrupts man's taste for the "living
water." Sin, sickness and disease are the spiritual and
physical conditions of those who drink from the wrong
source of water.**
The second Adam, Jesus, provided the answers for overcoming
consciousness through relying on the Holy Spirit. Those who

139

desire the "new birth" must be born from the water and Spirit. Creation and the new birth are the same and will produce the life and light of men. The spirit of man must enter the Spirit of Christ to be *born again.* There are no formulas or reciting of scriptures, which will produce this reality in ones life. i agree

The invisible world is reality. The "living water" of heaven manifested the everlasting Kingdom on earth to all who desired to drink. Faith is the living Word and developed through drinking Him not repeating scripture.

He established the eternal Kingdom, which transcends both the visible and invisible dimensions. **Man is a spiritual being who has been in a coma for centuries but has not died.**

The Word is life and light and if it becomes the steady diet of our spirits, it will produce the same image and likeness. Baptism is both spiritual and physical and "marks" those forever who are His disciples. **The power of being immersed into each character and person of the Godhead is one of the profound truths the devil has veiled with religion.**

Jesus demonstrated The Kingdom of heaven on earth and instructed His disciples to do the same. He described how to be *born again* and left instructions on baptism. If you are *born again* you are His disciple and your inheritance is to do greater works.

The plans of God have been completed in Christ and the only way we can live unattached in this world is with His mind. The Body of Christ will always have a remnant in the earth. We long to see the next generation operate in the "greater works." yes and

For me, the Bible is a door to experiences outside time and

space. Recently, the Holy Spirit showed me an open vision, which literally transported me to the feelings and experiences Jesus was battling before the cross. The sensation was so strong and "real" that I almost lost consciousness. Jesus would not allow thoughts from the physical dimension to enter His mind. He was able to discern the thoughts of men because of His position in God.

The power of the enemy is to capture our thoughts and focus them on our past or future. Once you understand that strategy you will be vigilant not to trust images in your mind or feelings in your body. *Amy ci agree*

The Holy Spirit will destroy the voices of fear and replace them with thoughts of victory. Death will loose its sting along with the images you once believed were real.

The authority of Christ is absolute and final and you must not confuse His crucifixion with weakness. Jesus used the cross to destroy death and hell. **He is asking you to take your place in Him and leave your past and future on the cross.** *Amen*

FINAL THOUGHTS

My experiences have just begun and these revelations are to provoke you to do whatever is necessary to enter Christ. Do not be content or distracted by your circumstances. You have what it takes to be *born again*!

If you are hungry and thirsty develop a relationship with the Holy Spirit. He responds to worship and thanksgiving. The time spent pursuing the Holy Spirit will be multiplied back 1000 fold. He is the one with access to our King and He shares the secrets of The Kingdom with those He trusts.

He is more precious to me than anything in my life. Upon waking my first thoughts are about Him and if He is absent I immediately begin to repent for any thoughts or actions, which may have offended Him.

My consciousness of Christ has changed dramatically because of Him and if your desire is to please Him nothing will be impossible. The adventure for eternity begins once you enter Christ.

Are you thirsty yet? **Nothing is impossible to those who drink from Him and become Immersed In Him.**

The [Holy] Spirit and the bride (the church, the true Christians) say, Come! And let him who is listening say, Come! And let everyone come who is thirsty [who is painfully conscious of his need of those things by which the soul is refreshed, supported, and strengthened]; and whoever [earnestly] desires to do it, let him come, take, appropriate, and drink the water of Life without cost.

Revelation 22:17 AMP

EVERLASTING TO EVERLASTING

If you enjoyed reading this book, we also recommend

The Last Adam

Who Has Bewitched You?

The Breath of God Over Essential Oils

Quantum Fasting

Participate in our courses live and

On Demand

Watch us on Frequencies of Glory TV
and follow us on Facebook

www.frequenciesofglorytv.com

www.facebook.com/EmersonFerrell
www.facebook.com/VoiceoftheLight

Contact our ministry at:

Voice of The Light Ministries
P.O. Box 3418
Ponte Vedra, FL. 32004
USA
904-834-2447

www.voiceofthelight.com

Made in United States
North Haven, CT
15 March 2024

50029043R00085